*Routledge Library Editions*

# INTERNATIONAL MONETARY CO-OPERATION

ECONOMICS

# INTERNATIONAL ECONOMICS
## In 11 Volumes

| | | |
|---|---|---|
| I | Applied Economics | *Brown* |
| II | Introduction to the World Economy | *Brown* |
| III | Economic Analysis and the Multinational Enterprise | *Dunning* |
| IV | Economic Survey | *Lewis* |
| V | International Monetary Economics | *Machlup* |
| VI | Problems of Economic Union | *Meade* |
| VII | An International Economic System | *Polak* |
| VIII | Britain in the World Economy | *Robertson* |
| IX | Economic Theory and Western European Integration | *Scitovsky* |
| X | International Monetary Co-Operation | *Tew* |
| XI | An Outline of International Price Theories | *Wu* |

# INTERNATIONAL MONETARY CO-OPERATION

## 1945-52

BRIAN TEW

Routledge
Taylor & Francis Group
LONDON AND NEW YORK

First published in 1952

Reprinted in 2003 by
Routledge
2 Park Square, Milton Park, Abingdon, Oxon, OX14 4RN
or
270 Madison Avenue, New York, NY 10016

First issued in paperback 2010

*Routledge is an imprint of the Taylor & Francis Group*



*British Library Cataloguing in Publication Data*
A CIP catalogue record for this book
is available from the British Library

International Monetary Co-Operation
ISBN 978-0-415-31365-0 (hbk)
ISBN 978-0-415-60741-4 (pbk)
ISBN 978-0-415-31355-1 (set)

Miniset: International Economics

Series: Routledge Library Editions – Economics

# INTERNATIONAL MONETARY CO-OPERATION

## 1945-52

*by*

BRIAN TEW
B.SC. (ECON.), PH.D.

PROFESSOR OF ECONOMICS,
UNIVERSITY OF NOTTINGHAM

Routledge
Taylor & Francis Group
LONDON AND NEW YORK

*First Published* - 1952

# CONTENTS

PART TWO

## MACHINERY OF INTERNATIONAL MONETARY CO-OPERATION



PART THREE

## THE COURSE OF EVENTS SINCE THE WAR

## LIST OF TABLES

## ABBREVIATIONS ETC. USED

| | |
|---|---|
| B.I.S. | Bank for International Settlements. |
| E.C.A. | Economic Co-operation Administration. |
| E.C.E. | Economic Commission for Europe. |
| E.P.U. | European Payments Union. |
| G.A.T.T. | General Agreement on Tariffs and Trade. |
| I.E.P.S. | Intra-European Payments Scheme. |
| I.M.F. | International Monetary Fund. |
| I.T.O. | International Trade Organization. |
| O.E.E.C. | Organization for European Economic Co-operation. |

One billion=1,000 millions.

# PREFACE

This book treats the theory and practice of international monetary co-operation, with special reference to the problems which have arisen since the last war, and the institutions which have been developed to meet them. No prior technical knowledge is expected of the reader, but an elementary knowledge of the relevant parts of economic theory will be found helpful. A suitable introduction to the subject would be Roy Harrod's *International Economics* or my own *Wealth and Income.*[1]

*International Monetary Co-operation* was written mainly in the first half of 1951, but amendments to the proofs have kept it up to date, and throughout the text 'now' can be taken to mean 'January 1952'. If my closing date had been a little later I would have mentioned in Chapter VII the recent United Nations' report on *Measures for International Economic Stability*, and in Chapter XI the latest *Economic Survey of Europe*[2] (which gives a remarkably good account of the course of international payments since the devaluations of September 1949). As it is, I can only suggest that the reader should himself consult these publications.

I wish to record my great indebtedness to the officials in the I.M.F., the O.E.E.C., the E.C.E., the E.C.A., and elsewhere, who went to so much trouble to assist my researches. I must, however, stress that I alone am responsible for any errors of fact and that the conclusions I have drawn commit no one else. My thanks are also due to Messrs. W. Beckerman, J. F. Brothwell and D. S. Lees, and to my wife, all of whom read my drafts and made valuable suggestions.

BRIAN TEW.

Nottingham.
*February* 1952.

[1]See the reading list below, page 175.
[2]*Economic Survey of Europe in* 1951, published by the E.C.E.

# *PART ONE*

# *FIRST PRINCIPLES*

CHAPTER I

## INTER-COUNTY PAYMENTS

I AM an inhabitant of a country, the United Kingdom, and as such I cannot but be aware that I and my fellow countrymen are collectively concerned—and, to judge by the pronouncements of statesmen and financial journalists, very deeply concerned—with certain problems of international payments, problems arising for example when we make and receive payments for the goods and services we buy from and sell to other countries or when we borrow and lend abroad. In the first place, we from time to time become anxious lest we should collectively suffer the embarrassment of running short of the means of settling our accounts with the rest of the world as a whole or with certain so-called 'hard-currency' countries in particular. This problem may be described as one of *external liquidity*. Then our anxiety is increased when we contemplate the difficulties involved in removing the causes of such an embarrassment. This second source of anxiety is, in technical terms, a matter of correcting an *external disequilibrium*. (A disequilibrium may be either a surplus or a deficit, but deficits are more important as a source of anxiety.) Lastly, we are aware that our internal level of business activity and employment is influenced by the inward and outward flows of payments which arise from our exports and imports of goods and services: in other words we are aware of the problem of the *employment effects* of such payments. Consequently, if we are suffering a depression, or if we fear one in the future, we are inclined to favour policies which promote exports and discourage imports. Since our imports are someone else's exports, and vice versa, such an inclination may be somewhat loosely described as a resolve not to import other countries' unemployment, amounting in some cases to a desire to export our own unemployment.

I am also an inhabitant of a sub-division of the United Kingdom, the county of Nottingham. I and my fellow inhabitants of this county, to whom for convenience I shall apply the label 'Nottspeople', frequently make payments to, and receive payments from, the inhabitants of the rest of the world, so that Nottinghamshire, no less than the United Kingdom, has somehow or other to settle her accounts with the rest of the world, to suffer changes in circumstances which may lead to external disequilibria, and to suffer also unemployment which may have been imported and could possibly be exported. Yet no one seems to consider these matters as worthy of attention, let alone as cause for anxiety. No industrious statisticians attempt to calculate the size or composition of Nottinghamshire's receipts and payments, no morbid economists draw depressing conclusions from the trend of Nottinghamshire's exports, no anxious statesman designates Lincolnshire or Yorkshire a hard-currency area. How are we to account for such a state of indifference?

### *The Problem of External Liquidity*

So far as external liquidity is concerned, the most obvious circumstance which distinguishes payments into and out of Nottinghamshire from payments into and out of the United Kingdom is that Nottinghamshire does not have a distinctive currency of her own but instead has a single currency in common with all other British counties, and this currency (sterling) can be transferred without restriction from one county to another. This arrangement has two important features. First, Nottinghamshire has a completely effective means of multilateral settlement with other counties: receipts obtained from any one county can be used for making payments to any other county. Second, Nottspeople always have the means of external settlement if they have the means of settling with each other, since the two media are identical.

*The Problem of External Disequilibrium*

The worst that could happen, if Nottspeople persistently spent more in the rest of Britain than the inhabitants of the rest of Britain spent in Nottinghamshire, would be that Nottspeople would eventually run out of money; their holdings of notes and bank deposits would be depleted and ultimately exhausted. In practice such a depletion of cash has never occurred on a scale sufficient to attract attention to the problem, but if a considerable depletion did occur the consequences would be serious, since if Nottspeople ran out of cash they would have nothing to spend and in consequence there would be local depression and unemployment. Such an outcome would represent an extreme manifestation of uncorrected external disequilibrium.

It may perhaps be thought that business depressions which Nottinghamshire has suffered in the past may have been due to a shortage of cash, which the inhabitants of Nottinghamshire stupidly failed to notice at the time. However, such a diagnosis of past depressions overlooks two important facts:

> First, if Nottspeople are on balance paying out cash, other counties must be receiving it. Hence, a depletion of cash holdings in Nottinghamshire, due to an excess of external payments over receipts, would not account for a *general* depression affecting the whole of Britain, and past depressions have in practice almost always affected all counties, though admittedly with unequal severity.
>
> Second, even purely local depressions may well not be attributable to a shortage of cash. Nobody need spend his money if he does not want to, and there are many reasons why spending might fall off in a particular county, apart from a shortage of cash. There is for instance no evidence that the decline in expenditure in the 'Depressed Areas' of the 1930s was attributable to a shortage of cash in these areas.

It will shortly be argued that there are corrective forces which would come into play long before Nottspeople's aggregate cash holdings became so depleted as to cause an increase in unemployment, but first it must be made clear that even a mild local depression is itself an appreciable corrective to any cash outflow from the county. For unemployed workers and impoverished businessmen are poor customers, and in particular are poor customers for goods produced over the county boundary, so that any diminution in the prosperity of Nottinghamshire, compared with that of other counties, would produce a rapid contraction in Nottinghamshire's imports from, and payments to, other counties. Here then is a powerful corrective to any outflow of money, but it is a very unsatisfactory remedy, since it involves a local depression. Happily, however, with reasonable luck, the nasty medicine need never be taken, except perhaps in small doses, for other forces are at work to correct the shortage of cash.

In the first place, Nottspeople own a large amount of securities which may or may not have originated in the county but which can be sold at any time on the stock exchanges. If the purchaser of the securities is not a Nottsperson—as is likely if Nottspeople are getting short of money—the sale of any of these securities represents a transfer of cash to Nottinghamshire from the rest of the country. In much the same way, Nottspeople may remedy a shortage of money by borrowing from Nottinghamshire branches of the nation-wide joint stock banks. Many Nottspeople are sufficiently credit-worthy to qualify for overdrafts at their bank, and an overdraft granted represents so much more money at the disposal of Nottspeople. Moreover, Nottinghamshire businesses in need of money may issue new securities, whether debentures or shares, and sell them to the British public at large, including that part of the British public which lives outside Nottinghamshire, and Nottinghamshire local authorities may likewise borrow from the British public at large.

The ability of Nottspeople to borrow or sell securities—whether old ones or new ones—over the county boundary, is facilitated by two factors: first, the existence of a common currency—sterling—throughout Britain is a great help, for all loans and securities are promises of money in the future, and investors commonly prefer promises of the type of money with which they are familiar; and second, neither Nottinghamshire nor any other British county imposes restrictions on capital transactions (whether in loans or securities) between one county and another or on the payment of interest or dividends over a county boundary.

These two factors, taken together, ensure that when Nottinghamshire has an export surplus (an excess of exports of goods and services to other counties over imports from other counties) Nottinghamshire investors use much of the resulting inflow of cash for buying sterling securities, and that both these accumulated securities and also newly issued ones can be readily sold outside Nottinghamshire, if ever the tide of trade should turn. There can be little doubt that the free flow of borrowing and lending between one county and another, particularly in the form of movements of securities, is a great benefit to the British people as a whole and to each single county. Counties with export surpluses of goods will almost inevitably contain people with money to invest; counties with import surpluses will almost inevitably contain people wishing to borrow or to sell their securities. What could be better than that the two parties should get together and undertake transactions which are to their own personal advantage and which, from a national point of view, perform the valuable service of promoting the even distribution of money throughout the country?

If, therefore, we wish to understand why Nottinghamshire can so readily find the means of settling her accounts with other counties, and of doing so on a multilateral basis, and can in addition so readily correct disequilibria between her receipts from, and payments to, other counties, we should bear in mind these aspects of the county's economic health: first, a common currency and banking system with the rest of Britain and second, the absence of restrictions on capital transactions.

### *The Problem of the Transmission of Business Depressions*

Thus far, then, Nottinghamshire's indifference to problems of inter-county payments seems to be justified on the ground that the problems so far considered are much less serious for Nottinghamshire than for the United Kingdom, but when we pass to our last problem, that of the employment effects of such payments, this particular ground for indifference is entirely absent. For Nottinghamshire is a completely open economy. Without tariffs, quotas, exchange controls, or any restrictions on transactions with other counties, Nottinghamshire has no means of resisting the import of unemployment or of favouring the export of unemployment. Nottspeople are aware that this is so, but accept the situation as it is, on account of the political and social solidarity which they feel towards other British people. Because of this solidarity, Nottspeople would regard it as illegitimate to attempt to export their depressions to neighbouring counties; moreover they regard a depression in another part of Britain as a disease which needs to be cured, not simply isolated. If each British county were a sovereign state, things would probably be otherwise. Nottspeople might then think it permissible to adopt 'beggar-my-neighbour' remedies for unemployment, and even if they fell short of that degree of irresponsibility they might well take the line that unemployment in Lancashire and Yorkshire was solely the private affair of Lancspeople and Yorkspeople and that, if the people directly concerned failed to cure their own malady, it was proper that Nottspeople should safeguard their own interests by insulating themselves from the source of infection, for example by imposing new tariffs.

*Conclusion*

The example of Nottinghamshire is instructive for two reasons. First, it serves to show why specifically inter-*national* payments present special problems which require separate study, and second, it represents a small-scale model whose efficiency of working would be regarded by many economists as an appropriate measuring rod for judging the efficiency of international monetary arrangements.

It is the aim of the next four chapters to explain in general terms the specifically international problems which arise when we transfer our attention from Nottinghamshire to an independent country such as the United Kingdom. One characteristic of independent countries in practice is that each has its own currency, so that great importance attaches to the terms and conditions on which one currency may be exchanged for another. This question is treated in Chapter II. When an economy has a separate currency, this currency will normally be in widespread use for making payments within the economy, but it is most unlikely to enjoy widespread acceptability as a means of payment outside the economy. Hence for such an economy there arises the question of the availability of means of settling with other economies—the question of international liquidity, which is the subject of Chapter III. Next, in Chapter IV, we have to consider the remedies which are available to a country whose means of international settlement are becoming unduly depleted—i.e. the remedies for a persistent international disequilibrium. Finally, there remains the question of how the tendency for business depressions to spread from one economy to another is regarded by the governments of the economies concerned when each economy is a sovereign state and not merely a minor political sub-division like Nottinghamshire. This question will be considered in Chapter V.

CHAPTER II

# EXCHANGE RATES

THOUGH it is impossible to point to a good present-day example of an international monetary system comparable with the inter-county monetary system described in the previous chapter, we can nevertheless find a reasonably good historical example if we go back to the gold currency standard of the nineteenth century. It may therefore be useful to state briefly the basic principles on which this standard operated, even though space does not permit reference to many important complications and imperfections which overlay these basic principles in practice.[1]

In order that there may be no confusion between our statement of the basic principles of the standard and the standard as it actually existed, let us imagine a purely hypothetical case and assume the British counties each to have a separate gold currency and all to adhere to the rules of the gold currency standard. Each county, then, has an internal currency comprising its own distinctive gold coins—the 'Nottscrown', the 'Cornish sovereign', and so on—the manufacture of which is exclusively in the hands of the county's official mint. However, each county's mint, though a monopolist, is prepared to mint coins (for a small commission) for anyone supplying the necessary gold. In addition holders of coins are quite free to melt them down into bars, so that both coins and bar gold are readily convertible into one another. Thus to the extent that gold can be freely transported from one county to another—a necessary condition for the efficient working of the system—

[1]One of the complications which we shall ignore is that Britain and other countries adhering to the gold currency standard usually had a second type of internal currency in the form of paper money, i.e. of bank-notes and bank deposits. Moreover, as we shall see in Chapter IX, English paper money (sterling) acted in effect as an alternative to gold for making international payments, so that the so-called gold standard was in practice a gold-cum-sterling standard.

inter-county payments can always be made in gold, which is at the same time the normal means of making payments within each county. Admittedly, inter-county payments in gold are a little more troublesome than internal payments, because they involve the cost of melting down and re-minting and also of transporting the gold for a longer distance, but apart from this complication there would be in effect a single currency in use throughout the whole of Britain, just as there is in real life: this common currency would however in our imaginary example be gold, whereas in real life it is a paper currency, sterling.

But let us now consider the consequences of the expense involved in reminting and long-distance transport whenever payments are made from one county to another by actually sending gold. Let us suppose, for example, that though the Nottscrown has the same gold content as the Hantscrown, a Nottsperson needing to pay 100 Hantscrowns to a creditor in Hampshire would have to melt down 105 Nottscrowns in order to provide the necessary margin for expenses, and that for similar reasons 100 Hantscrowns melted down and sent to Nottingham, would yield, net of expenses, only 95 Nottscrowns. In these circumstances Nottspeople and Hantspeople would be pleased to find an alternative way of making payments to each other, and happily an alternative way is available, namely that of exchanging coins. If, for example, Mr. A in Nottingham needs to pay Mr. B in Southampton, while Mr. C in Southampton needs to pay Mr. D in Nottingham, the costs of melting, reminting and transport could be avoided if Mr. A put his Nottscrowns at Mr. C's disposal in Nottingham, in exchange for Mr. C's putting Hantscrowns at Mr. A's disposal in Southampton, thereby enabling Mr. C. to pay Mr. D in Nottscrowns and Mr. A to pay Mr. B in Hantscrowns. Such a procedure would, however, give rise to a phenomenon which is *not* found in real life in the British internal monetary system, the phenomenon of an exchange rate between the currencies in use in different parts of the country, for Mr. A must have bought Hantscrowns with Nottscrowns by exchanging so many Hantscrowns per 100 Nottscrowns. It should however be noted that under the gold currency standard the exchange rate between any two currencies is closely determined by the relative gold contents of the two types of coin. Thus in our example, where the two coins (the Nottscrown and the Hantscrown) are supposed to have the same gold content, the exchange rate between the two will never differ greatly from 100 Hantscrowns=100 Nottscrowns. More precisely, on the assumptions we have made, the exchange rate will always lie between 100 Hantscrowns=95 Nottscrowns and 100 Hantscrowns=105 Nottscrowns, for if the exchange rate lay outside these limits it would be more advantageous for one of the parties concerned to send gold rather than make an exchange transaction.

In brief, then, though the phenomenon of exchange rates clearly arose under the gold currency standard, these rates were closely determined by the gold contents of the different countries' internal currencies. When however we come to consider the conditions prevailing in the world of the present day, when the internal currencies of virtually all countries are bank-notes and promises of bank-notes,[1] the monetary material itself, being merely paper, obviously has no significance in the determination of the relative values of different national currencies. What then does determine the exchange rates between different paper currencies? Let us tackle this question by first considering the facilities which exist for exchanging one paper currency for another.

The simplest way in which exchange facilities can be arranged is for the government of each country to adopt a *laissez-faire* policy and allow its nationals to buy and sell foreign currencies against the home currency, without official intervention or restriction of any kind. Under such a regime, competitive markets grow up in which each currency is exchanged against every other currency, and a single market price, or exchange rate, comes to obtain as between every possible pair of currencies. Since *laissez-faire* implies that residents in any country may deal freely with foreigners as well as with their fellow countrymen, the market price of any one currency in terms of any other will tend to be uniform not only within each country but over the whole world. For if,

[1]Apart from small change in the form of token coins which have a metallic value considerably below their face value, and which are not freely minted.

say, the price of £1 were \$4 in London but \$3 in New York, all buyers of sterling for dollars would try to buy in New York, which would bid up the New York price of sterling, while all sellers of sterling for dollars would try to sell in London, which would depress the London price of sterling, and this process would continue until the two rates had achieved virtual equality.

Moreover, not only would *laissez-faire* result in the exchange rate between any pair of currencies being uniform throughout the world, but arbitrage operations would ensure that the rates established for different pairs of currencies would be 'orderly', in the sense that the 'direct' rate between any pair of currencies, A and B, (i.e. the rate at which currency A was actually being exchanged for currency B) would never differ appreciably from the 'cross rate' implied by the two direct rates (i) between A and some third currency and (ii) between B and the same third currency. A hypothetical example will make this point clear. Let us suppose that under *laissez-faire* the direct pound-dollar rate happened to be £1=\$4 and the direct pound-franc rate £1=Fr. 1,000, the implied cross rate thus being \$1=Fr. 250. Let us also suppose, however, that (for some reason which need not concern us here) the direct dollar-franc rate was not \$1=Fr. 250 but \$1=Fr. 200. It would then be profitable for me to undertake the following arbitrage operation. Beginning with a capital of £100, I could exchange it for Fr. 100,000 (at the direct rate of £1=Fr. 1,000), then exchange my Fr. 100,000 for \$500 (at the direct rate of \$1=Fr. 200), and finally exchange my \$500 for £125 (at the direct rate of £1=\$4), thus making £25 profit on the operation. I and my fellow operators could profitably continue such transactions so long as the direct rates remained 'disorderly'. But as the result of the continuous bidding with sterling for francs, the sterling price of francs would tend to rise, and likewise the franc price of dollars and the dollar price of sterling. In this way an orderly pattern of direct rates would rapidly establish itself.

Though under *laissez-faire* exchange rates would be uniform throughout the world and orderly, they would not of course be stable. If, for example, British people suddenly decided to buy more goods from overseas, a necessary preliminary would be for them to use their sterling to bid for increased quantities of foreign currencies, and this would have the effect of raising the sterling prices of these currencies, or (to put the same thing in a different way) of causing sterling to depreciate in relation to other currencies. Moreover sterling would go on depreciating until the balance of demand and supply was restored, either by the rising sterling prices of overseas currencies choking off the increased British demand for them, or by the increasing cheapness of sterling inducing foreigners to spend more of their currencies on purchasing sterling. Now, as we shall later see,[1] the conditions under which international trade is at present conducted are such that the short-run effect of a depreciation of any one currency, say sterling, may be to cause foreigners to spend less, rather than more, of their currencies on buying sterling, while the curtailment of British demand for foreign currencies may well occur rather slowly. Hence in practice a very large fluctuation in exchange rates may be required to maintain the balance of demand and supply, following an initial disturbance.

The instability of exchange rates under *laissez-faire* would be aggravated by speculation. If for example the view became widespread that sterling was about to depreciate, there would be a rush by holders of sterling to exchange it for other currencies; this would bring about the expected depreciation, whether or not it would have occurred in any case. Thus a widely believed rumour, even if lacking any substantial foundation, would tend to justify itself, and consequently to gain added credence, and there might therefore occur variations in exchange rates which could be described as partially or even wholly self-generating.

The great instability of exchange rates which would be liable to arise under *laissez-faire*, and the great inconvenience which would occur as a result, have been almost universally held to justify either official transactions in the exchange markets, or official restrictions on private exchange transactions, or a combination of both.

With official transactions but no official restrictions, exchange rates tend towards uniformity and orderliness, as

[1]Page 56, footnote 1.

under *laissez-faire*, the only departure from *laissez-faire* being that the monetary authorities[1] of the countries concerned undertake exchange transactions themselves, with the object of offsetting, partially or wholly, variations in exchange rates which otherwise would have occurred. An extreme case of official intervention of this kind was the gold *bullion* standard, the form in which the gold standard was restored after a hiatus caused by the First World War. Under the gold bullion standard, the monetary authorities of each of the countries adhering to the standard undertook to buy and sell gold bullion against the country's internal paper currency in unlimited quantities at a fixed price.[2] Adherence to the gold bullion standard thus required that each country's monetary authorities should hold a reserve of gold, which they would add to or deplete according to circumstances, and the consequence of the standard was that the value of each country's currency was fixed within narrow limits in relation to gold (and thus in relation to each other country's currency), in much the same way as under the gold currency standard, so long as none of the countries was forced off the standard by the exhaustion of its gold reserve.

Under the gold bullion standard any international disequilibrium would, if sufficiently prolonged, eventually exhaust the gold reserve of the deficit countries, so that under this standard the question of dealing with such deficits was liable to pose itself in a rather dramatic form. The remedies which a country might adopt to deal with a persistent deficit, while continuing to maintain unchanged the gold value of its currency, we shall consider in Chapter IV; but sometimes these remedies were so unattractive or impracticable that the countries concerned did in fact abandon the standard. A case in point was

[1]The institutions which should be classified as a country's monetary authorities differ slightly from country to country, but in all cases would include the central government and the central bank. In Britain the monetary authorities can best be taken as the Government, the central bank (the Bank of England) and the joint stock banks. On this point, see my *Wealth and Income*, Chapter 10.

[2]This is a slight over-simplification, since the buying and selling rates were slightly different, to provide a small commission. In England the official purchase price was 77/9d. a standard ounce and the official selling price 77/10½d.

the abandonment of the gold standard by Britain in September 1931.

Britain's defection from the gold standard is interesting from our point of view in that it led to the development of a technique of *partial* stabilization of a currency (in this case sterling) by official transactions. After September 1931 the British monetary authorities did not commit themselves to maintain a fixed gold value of the pound, but instead they set themselves the task of 'ironing out' short term fluctuations, which (as we have noted) might well have been very large under a regime of complete *laissez-faire*. The new policy was carried out by the Exchange Equalization Account, which was created in 1932 and thereafter administered by the Bank of England on behalf of the British Treasury. The Account was given an initial stock of sterling assets in the form of British Treasury Bills (which are in effect IOUs which the Bank of England is always prepared to exchange for new English paper money). The Account used its sterling assets to buy gold and foreign currencies whenever the pound seemed to be appreciating excessively; in doing so it increased the supply of sterling and thus depressed its value. Later on, when the Account had by such transactions accumulated a substantial stock of gold and foreign currencies, it was able to operate on a two-way basis and either exchange its sterling for gold and foreign currencies (when the pound appreciated excessively) or exchange its gold and foreign currencies for sterling (when the pound depreciated excessively).

A country's monetary authorities can, then, either determine or (less ambitiously) merely influence the external value of their own paper currency simply by undertaking transactions in the foreign exchange markets, provided that their stocks of gold and foreign currencies do not become exhausted. We have still to consider the much more drastic technique which can be used to the same ends, that of exchange control, or the official restriction of private exchange transactions. Exchange control may be imposed either on payments or on receipts or (more usually) on both. The present British exchange control, which is on both payments and receipts, dates back to the beginning of the Second World War. In the preceding inter-war period, exchange control had been comparatively rare, except in the case of the U.S.S.R. and of Germany and her allies.

Exchange control on payments usually takes the form that all purchases of gold or of foreign paper currencies (or of certain types of claims to foreign currencies) against the home currency need to be licensed by the home monetary authorities, who are given power to restrict, or even stop altogether, the issue of licences for particular types of transactions, such as the purchase of certain (or all) foreign currencies to pay for so-called 'luxury' imports or to buy foreign securities. In its effects exchange control on payments corresponds very closely to quotas or prohibitions on the import of goods, since foreign currencies are bought *inter alia* as a preliminary to buying foreign goods. Hence restrictions on the purchase of foreign currencies can be made to reduce imports of goods just as effectively as import restrictions, while conversely restrictions on imports are an effective device for curtailing the demand for foreign currencies. Thus it is frequently only a matter of administrative convenience whether a given aim is attained by exchange control or by import quotas or prohibitions. The only cases where the two devices are not alternatives are where the purchase of a foreign currency would be associated with a purchase not of goods but of services or of securities or other capital assets. If for example I wish to buy dollars for the purpose of spending a holiday in America (where I would buy the services of American hotels etc.) or of buying U.S. government bonds, I cannot be restrained by import quotas or prohibitions, since I do not propose to import any American goods into this country, but I shall nevertheless be thwarted if the British exchange control refuses my application for a licence to buy dollars. An exchange control on payments is thus rather more comprehensive in its scope than are quotas and prohibitions on imports of goods.

Exchange control on receipts is usually imposed, not to reduce exports or to prevent exporters from selling the foreign currencies they earn, but to force any home resident who obtains foreign currencies to sell them to the home monetary authorities. To this end it is usually made illegal for any home resident to hold gold, foreign currencies, or certain types of claims to foreign currencies, except under licence, and licences are issued only at the discretion of the authorities. The purpose of this kind of exchange control (which since the war has been enforced more or less strictly by almost all countries) is simply to centralize a country's means of external payment in a common pool, in the hands of the monetary authorities.

In many cases exchange controls are enforced by suppressing the free markets in gold and foreign currencies, or at any rate in certain foreign currencies, and giving the monetary authorities the position of monopolistic dealer in all transactions in the currencies concerned. The authorities are then able to impose any terms they deem appropriate on any home resident wishing to buy or sell the foreign currencies in question. Alternatively the free market may not be suppressed but merely restricted, only certain classes of purchasers and sellers being allowed access to the free market.

The suppression of free dealings makes it possible for the monetary authorities to act as a *discriminating* monopolist in fixing exchange rates or, in the words of the International Monetary Fund Agreement,[1] to indulge in 'multiple currency practices'. They may quote widely different buying and selling rates for the same foreign currency, and also different buying (selling) rates according to the type of international transaction giving rise to the supply of (demand for) a particular currency. Even the restriction, as distinct from the suppression, of free dealings may facilitate multiple currency practices, in that it may give rise to two exchange rates for the same currency, the official rate, applicable to certain transactions, and the so-called 'free' rate, applicable to others. A good example of multiple currency practices is provided by Chile, whose exchange rates in 1950 are set out in Table 1 at the end of this chapter.

Just as the official licensing of overseas payments corresponds broadly to quotas or prohibitions on the import of goods, so multiple currency practices correspond broadly to the imposition of tariffs (i.e. customs duties) on imported goods. If, for example, the Australian monetary authorities suddenly abandoned their traditional policy of buying and selling sterling

[1] See below, Chapter VI.

at virtually the same price in Australian pounds (at present approximately £100 Stg.=£125 Australian), and imposed a higher selling price of £100 Stg.=£150 Australian, this would mean that Australian purchasers would have to pay to the Australian authorities a levy of £25 Australian on every 100 English pounds' worth of goods imported, in exactly the same manner as if the Australian government had imposed an all-round 20 per cent *ad valorem* tariff on all imports. If a third exchange rate of £100 Stg.=£250 Australian were imposed in respect of the overseas currency requirements of importers of 'luxury' goods, this would correspond to a new 100 per cent tariff on such goods. In other cases multiple exchange rates are equivalent in their effects to export taxes or subsidies. Thus if the Australian authorities began to enforce a new *buying* rate of £100 Stg.=£100 Australian in respect of the overseas earnings of wool exporters, this would correspond to an export tax on wool, while had the rate been £100 Stg.=£175 Australian this would have been the equivalent of an export subsidy on wool.

The suppression of free exchange markets, or even simply the suppression of arbitrage transactions, may also cause a divergence between the direct exchange rate between two currencies and the implied cross rate between them. As we have seen, so long as free dealings are permitted by all countries, private arbitrage operations ensure that the three direct exchange rates between any three currencies, A, B and C, are such that the cross rate between B and C implied by the direct rates between A and B and between A and C cannot differ appreciably from the direct rate between B and C. This multilateral orderliness of exchange rates is not affected by official transactions by the monetary authorities, but it can readily be upset by exchange control, with consequences which will be made clear by the example given below on page 71.

There is considerable scope for international co-operation in the field of exchange rates once it is agreed that there is any case for departing from strict *laissez-faire*. First, there is a minimum need for bilateral agreements on direct rates between each country and every other country, simply to ensure that the monetary authorities of two countries do not act at cross purposes and attempt to stabilize the same direct exchange rate at different levels. Second, unless the monetary authorities of the countries concerned are willing and able to enforce the very drastic exchange restrictions which are required effectively to prevent arbitrage operations, multilateral agreement is necessary to ensure that direct rates are settled on an orderly basis, with cross rates in conformity with the corresponding direct rates. Third, as we shall see in Chapter IV, there is need for international action to reduce restrictions on payments, whether these restrictions are exclusively outright prohibitions of certain payments or categories of payments, or whether they include also multiple currency practices.

## TABLE I

MULTIPLE EXCHANGE RATES IN OPERATION IN CHILE[1]

*All rates expressed in Pesos per U.S. Dollar*

| Buying Rate | Applicable to: | Selling Rate | Applicable to: |
|---|---|---|---|
| 19.37 | Local currency requirements of large foreign-owned mining companies for current operating costs. | | |
| | | 31.00 | (i) Essential imports of goods. (ii) Certain authorized imports of services. |
| 37.00 | Exports of such goods as hides, wool and fish products. | | |
| 39.40 | Agricultural and industrial exports, with certain exceptions. | | |
| 41.20 | Exports of wheat, beans, and produce of small mines. | | |
| 43.00 | (i) Exports such as sodium sulphate and some foodstuffs. (ii) Exports of services. (iii) Capital transactions, including local currency requirements for capital investments of large mining companies. | 43.10 | (i) Non-essential imports of goods. (ii) Other authorized imports of services. (iii) Capital transactions. |
| 100.77[2] | Local currency requirements of visiting tourists and diplomats. | 100.77[2] | Non-licensed imports of services. |
| 130.00[3] | Sales of newly mined gold. | 130.00[3] | Authorized imports of luxury goods. |

[1]Taken from page 98 of the I.M.F.'s *First Annual Report on Exchange Restrictions*, published in March 1950. Chile's exchange rates have been altered on several occasions since the *Report* appeared.

[2]Fluctuating free market rate.

[3]Fluctuating gold market rate.

## CHAPTER III

# INTERNATIONAL LIQUIDITY

### *The Means of International Settlement*

THE resources which are available to us for settling our accounts with other countries fall under three main headings. First, we may be able to settle in our own paper currency, though only to the extent that the rest of the world is prepared to accumulate our currency. In other terms, we can settle our international accounts in our own currency to the extent that we enjoy unused 'accumulation facilities' with other countries. Second, we can also settle our accounts by drawing on our own holdings of liquid international assets—gold, foreign currencies, and 'safe' short-term claims to foreign currencies. Third, we may enjoy external 'drawing rights', whether in the form of loans or credits (like the Anglo-American loan negotiated in 1945), which have eventually to be repaid in the currency of the lending country, or in the form of outright grants (like those made available by the United States under Marshall Aid).

Special importance attaches to a country's *official* resources under all three headings, since these represent the country's first line strength in circumstances when it is thought necessary to maintain the value of the home currency in terms of foreign currencies; unofficial holders of gold, foreign currencies, etc., may find it profitable to dispose of their holdings in the same circumstances, but in present day conditions they cannot be counted upon to do so, partly for the reasons outlined on pages 46-7, partly because their freedom of action is often limited by the wish to conceal their holdings from the exchange control authorities. Hence if we wish to consider a country's external liquidity it will almost always be correct to take into account only such means of settlement as are in the hands of the monetary authorities. The use of official resources, whether of liquid international assets, accumulation facilities, or drawing rights, for the purpose of stabilizing the external value of the home currency, may be called (in the terminology used by the International Monetary Fund) 'compensatory official financing'.

Accumulation facilities and drawing rights are of little value as means of external settlement unless they can be exercised quickly and are certain, or highly likely, to be available if required. Facilities of a kind which satisfy this criterion can with few exceptions be provided only by the official agencies of foreign governments or by an inter-governmental organization such as the International Monetary Fund.[1] It is usual for both accumulation facilities and drawing rights to be limited by prior agreement to a definite maximum, sometimes known as the 'swing', or alternatively the 'ceiling', of the agreement. There is however one circumstance in which accumulation facilities are neither the result of an agreement nor subject to a definite ceiling: this occurs when country A enjoys accumulation facilities with B by virtue of the fact that B has elected to adhere to A's currency as a standard, as for instance Australia and the other countries of the outer Sterling Area adhere to sterling as a standard, which means that B's monetary authorities follow a policy of offering to buy or sell A's currency without limit at a published price, just as countries on the gold bullion standard would always buy and sell gold at a published price. The accumulation facilities thereby offered by B to A would be limitless so long as B did not change her policy, which however she would be free to do on her own initiative.

It may be helpful at this stage to consider a practical example of compensatory official financing. Table 2A below sets out the receipts which came to the United Kingdom from overseas in 1946 and the payments made overseas by the United Kingdom in the same year. Some of the receipts and payments were on current, others on capital, account. Current receipts comprise the sales proceeds of goods and services sold overseas, income received on British-owned overseas investments, and (usually a negligible item) incomes paid as gifts to Britishers by foreigners. Current payments comprise payments for goods and services supplied from overseas, income paid to overseas owners of investments in Britain, and income paid overseas as

[1]The purchase rights which the I.M.F. affords its members are a special case of accumulation facilities. See Chapter VI.

gifts. The excess of current payments over current receipts, technically known as the United Kingdom's negative or 'unfavourable' *balance of current payments*, was (according to Table 2A) £230 millions in 1946.

The same table gives the balance of the capital items, excluding compensatory official financing, as unfavourable to the extent of £2 millions;[1] this amount added to the balance of current payments gives Britain's total *external deficit* for the year—£232 millions. As is shown in Table 2B, this deficit was financed to the extent of £38 millions by virtue of the accumulation facilities enjoyed by sterling in overseas countries and to the extent of £279 millions by virtue of borrowing facilities accorded to Britain by the United States and Canadian governments; the use of these facilities made it unnecessary to draw on the official reserve of liquid international assets, which indeed actually increased by £85 millions.

We may note at this point that the concepts introduced in Tables 2A and 2B represent a sophisticated version of some of the basic ideas already introduced in Chapter I with reference to Nottinghamshire. If the two tables had referred to Nottinghamshire, instead of to the United Kingdom, the chief current items in the first table would have been 'receipts from Nottinghamshire's exports of goods and services' (on the left-hand side) and 'payments for Nottinghamshire's imports of goods and services' (on the right-hand side). Then in the second part of the first table we would have found 'net borrowing by Notts-people from people outside the county' (corresponding to item 4) and a balancing item (corresponding to item 6). Finally, in the second table, this balancing item would be shown to correspond simply to the net amount of money transferred into or out of the county in the course of the year.

The greater sophistication which is required when considering an independent country's balance of payments unfortunately gives rise to a number of awkward statistical problems. The most important of these, for our present purposes, is that of distinguishing between 'compensatory official financing' and 'other capital items' in certain cases of

[1]Namely items 9, 10 and 11 (total £m. 201) minus items 4 and 5 (total £m. 199).

## TABLE 2A[1]

U.K. BALANCE OF PAYMENTS IN 1946
*(all figures in £ millions)*

CURRENT ITEMS

| *Receipts* | | *Payments* | |
|---|---|---|---|
| 1. Exports of goods[2] .. | 948 | 7. Imports of goods[2] .. | 1,033 |
| 2. Net income from shipping and other services sold overseas .. .. | 49 | 8. Government expenditure overseas .. .. | 263 |
| 3. Net income from overseas investments .. | 69 | | |
| Total current receipts | 1,066 | Total current payments | 1,296 |

CAPITAL ITEMS

| | | | |
|---|---|---|---|
| 4. Net private investment in U.K. by foreigners .. | 127 | 9. Government grants and loans for relief and rehabilitation and for civilian supplies to Germany .. .. | 142 |
| 5. Capital payments made by overseas countries to the U.K. government .. | 72 | 10. Repayment of loans and other capital payments by the U.K. government to the U.S.A. and Canada .. | 52 |
| 6. Balancing item (=external deficit) .. .. | 232 | 11. Gold subscriptions to the I.M.F. and International Bank .. | 7 |
| Grand Total .. | 1,497 | Grand Total .. | 1,497 |

## TABLE 2B[1]

U.K. COMPENSATORY OFFICIAL FINANCING IN 1946
*(all figures in £ millions)*

| | |
|---|---|
| Utilization of accumulation and borrowing facilities: | |
| Increase in sterling balances held overseas .. .. | 38 |
| Drawings on U.S. and Canadian credits .. .. .. | 279 |
| *Less*, increase in the U.K.'s official reserve of gold and foreign currencies .. .. .. .. .. .. .. | —85 |
| TOTAL .. .. | 232 |

[1]These two tables are taken from the I.M.F.'s second Balance of Payments Yearbook, published in 1950, page 383.

[2]Calculated at their value when loaded on board ship, i.e. net of all shipping costs.

official financing. In principle the criterion to be applied is one of motive: 'the distinguishing mark of a compensatory transaction is that it is undertaken broadly to balance international transactions during the reporting period',[1] whereas a non-compensatory transaction is one which is undertaken irrespective of the size of the surplus or deficit which would otherwise occur. A case in point is Marshall Aid. Was the primary aim of this Aid to relieve Europe's shortage of dollars by supplying gratis goods which otherwise would have had to be bought for dollars, or was it simply a relief measure which would have been undertaken even if the European countries had not been short of dollars? The answer is uncertain, but since the amount and the allocation of the Aid was based on estimates of the 'dollar gap' of each of the recipient countries, the presumption is that the United States intended it primarily as an act of compensatory financing. Such, at any rate, is the view of I.M.F. statisticians, on whose judgment we can rely with considerable confidence in such matters.

### *Multilateral Settlement in Conditions of Equilibrium*

Arrangements for international settlements range from the strictly bilateral to the fully multilateral. So long as no exchange controls exist, the exchange markets provide the necessary facilities for fully multilateral settlements, since the owner of any one currency can obtain any other currency simply by bidding for it. There therefore remains to consider only the kinds of arrangements which may prevail under a regime of exchange controls, such as exists today throughout the greater part of the world.[2]

Let us begin with the extreme case of complete bilateralism, which is unlikely to arise in practice unless the monetary authorities of either or both of the countries concerned enjoy a monopolistic status as dealer in the other's currency. In these particular circumstances a purely bilateral arrangement can be concluded, like the agreements made between the United Kingdom and various European countries soon after their liberation, consisting essentially of an agreement to fix the

[1]The I.M.F.'s second Balance of Payments Yearbook, page 23.
[2]See Chapter VII.

exchange rate between the two countries' currencies and to create accumulation facilities on either a one-way or a reciprocal basis. (Such agreements are described in Chapter VIII.)

A step towards multilateralism can be achieved on the basis of bilateral accumulation facilities if a group of countries, all of whom have bilateral agreements with one another, agree among themselves to undertake circular offsetting. This is possible and advantageous when facilities have been used in a closed circuit—for example if country A has been running a bilateral deficit with B, B with C and C with A—and when in addition the facilities are in each case subject to a risk of eventual exhaustion. In such a case the countries in the circuit will each find it advantageous if they can arrange that each one of them should write down its holding of the 'preceding' country's currency in return for a similar cancellation of its own currency in the hands of the following country in the circuit, the amount of each of the cancellations being equivalent in value to the smallest of the holdings in the circuit. For by virtue of the offsetting operation each country in the circuit would enjoy an increase in its outstanding accumulation facilities available for use against the following country in the circuit.

In the special case of world-wide international equilibrium, where each country's bilateral deficits are precisely balanced in total by its bilateral surpluses, it is possible to arrange all countries' bilateral deficits into a series of closed circuits, and to cancel the lot by circular offsetting.[1] Such a state of affairs corresponds perfectly to the ideal of international settlement on a fully multilateral basis, for if all deficits can be offset as they arise, or with only a short delay, no country has any reason to care with whom it runs deficits and with whom it runs surpluses, provided that (in conformity with our hypothesis) its deficits and surpluses are in overall balance. If however our perfect equilibrium gives way to disequilibrium, with some countries developing overall deficits and others

[1]See Ekker: *Equilibrium of International Trade and International Monetary Compensations*, in Weltwirtschaftliches Archiv, Band 64, Heft 2, 1950. This authoritative article provides the basis for many of the arguments in the remainder of this chapter, and should be consulted by readers who want a more rigorous exposition.

overall surpluses,[1] the proportion of deficits which can be arranged in closed circuits and offset undergoes a progressive decline. Disequilibria of the magnitude which have occurred in practice in the post-war world may well reduce the possible amount of circular offsetting to almost negligible proportions.[2]

Another device for facilitating settlements on a multilateral basis is that of transferable currencies. If for instance country A has acquired a stock of country X's currency, the monetary authorities of the latter country may refrain from placing any obstacle in the way of A using this currency to make payments to country B. In such a case X's currency qualifies as a 'transferable currency'. Transferability may be unconditional, as in the case of transfers of sterling between *any* countries before the last war, or it may be conditional. A conditionally transferable currency may be subject to conditions clearly laid down in advance (e.g. that the currency may not be transferred to finance capital transactions or payments to particular countries), in which case it may be said to enjoy conditional but automatic transferability; or it may be necessary for each transfer to be authorized by the exchange control authorities of the country issuing the currency, in which case the transferability is said to be discretionary or 'administrative'. (At the present time, as we shall see in Chapter IX, the transfer of sterling between different countries is in some cases unconditional, in other cases conditional and automatic, in yet other cases conditional on an administrative basis, and in still other cases completely prohibited.)

It is easy to see that circular transfers of X's currency could serve the same purpose as circular offsetting. For (to adapt our previous examples) suppose that X is Britain and that A's deficit with B, B's with C and C's with A are each the equivalent of £10 millions sterling. Then instead of each country using its bilateral accumulation facilities against the next country in the circuit, the status quo then being restored by circular offsetting,

[1]The total of the overall deficits of the deficit countries is of course necessarily equal to the total of the overall surpluses of the surplus countries, since overall deficits and surpluses are derived (by simple addition or subtraction) from bilateral deficits and surpluses, and what is a bilateral deficit to one country is a bilateral surplus to another.

[2]Ekker, op. cit.

it would be equally satisfactory if the circuit of deficits had been cleared by the payment of £10 millions sterling each from A to B, B to C and C to A. It therefore follows that, provided that each country is in overall equilibrium, circular transfers of one or more unconditionally transferable currencies can, like circular offsetting, provide a completely satisfactory means of achieving international settlement on a fully multilateral basis within a group of countries, but that the scope for such transfers is progressively curtailed to the extent that this condition is unfulfilled.

*Multilateral Settlement in Conditions of Disequilibrium*

To what extent, if at all, can settlement be achieved on a multilateral basis within a group of countries *not* in equilibrium, i.e. where some countries have overall deficits and others overall surpluses? Supposing that in such a group of countries in a given period[1] all closed circuits of bilateral deficits were eliminated, what deficits would remain and how could they be settled? This question can best be tackled as follows. It can be proved[2] that after all circular bilateral deficits have been eliminated, one country will necessarily emerge as having bilateral surpluses with some or all of the other countries and deficits with none. Let us call this the 'strongest' country.[3] There will also necessarily be a second strongest country with a bilateral deficit with the strongest country but with bilateral surpluses with all the other countries. Similarly a third strongest country will have bilateral deficits with the first and second strongest countries but surpluses with all the remaining

[1]The choice of an accounting period for calculating bilateral deficits is necessarily arbitrary. It should be noted that a lengthening of the accounting period may reduce, not increase, the bilateral deficit of one country with another: for example, A's deficit with B in January may be partially balanced by B having a deficit with A in February, in which case A's bilateral deficit for the two months together will be less than for January alone. The more months we consider at a time the more important is the cancelling out of 'reciprocal deficits' (as we call them in Chapter VIII) likely to be. See below, page 105.

[2]See Ekker, op. cit.

[3]The label 'strongest' is purely for purposes of identification and does not imply that it is praiseworthy to be 'strong'. For a somewhat similar use of the term, see Professor J. M. Fleming's article 'On Making the Best of Balance of Payments Restrictions on Imports' in the *Economic Journal*, March 1951.

countries. These remaining countries can in their turn be arranged in a definite order of 'strength', the weakest country having bilateral deficits with everybody else.

A numerical illustration will help to clarify this point. Suppose that there are only eight countries in the world: Canada, the U.S.A., the U.K., Britannica, Europa, Imperia, Latinnia and Miscellannia, and that we have estimated the bilateral balances obtaining between each of the 28 pairs of countries in some particular year. We could then present our estimates in the form of a table with each of the 28 bilateral estimates classified according to both the surplus partner and the deficit partner. If we did no more than this our entries would be scattered over the table without forming a simple pattern, but if in addition we eliminate all closed circuits of deficits and then arrange our countries in the order of their strength, we shall find, as in Table 3(A), that all the entries fall on one side of one of the diagonals, in the form of a compact 'wedge'.[1] The significance of this pattern of entries is that the settlements required to meet all the bilateral deficits represent a uni-directional flow from the weaker to the stronger countries. Thus the weakest country, Europa, has to settle bilateral deficits with the seven countries which are stronger than she is, Britannica with her six superiors in strength, the U.K. with her five superiors in strength, and so on, until we reach the strongest country, the U.S.A., with no deficits at all.

The summary table, Table 3(B), tells us that of the eight countries, three have overall surpluses, totalling $m 7,290, while the other five have overall deficits, which necessarily total the same amount.[2] The total of the 28 individual bilateral deficits (or surpluses), two of which are so small as to be

[1]The figures in Table 3 are actually taken from the first half of Table 88 of the E.C.E.'s *Economic Survey of Europe in* 1949, page 167, except that closed circuits have been eliminated and the names of imaginary countries substituted for certain groups of countries. Thus Latinnia corresponds to the Latin American republics, Britannica to the outer Sterling Area, and so on.

[2]It is not logically necessary that all countries with overall surpluses should in all circumstances be stronger than countries with overall deficits. If for example in Table 3(A) Europa's bilateral deficit with the U.K. had been 1,200 instead of 200, the appropriate order of the countries would be unchanged, but the U.K. would then have had an overall surplus, not an overall deficit.

## TABLE 3

### AN ILLUSTRATION OF THE PATTERN OF BILATERAL DEFICITS, WITH ALL CLOSED CIRCUITS OF DEFICITS ELIMINATED

*(The figures are expressed in millions of U.S. dollars, and relate to some particular year)*

### Table 3(A): The Individual Bilateral Deficits and Surpluses

| Countries with their bilateral Deficits | Countries with their bilateral Surpluses: | | | | | | | |
|---|---|---|---|---|---|---|---|---|
| | U.S.A. | Latinnia | Canada | Miscel-lannia | Imperia | U.K. | Brit-annica | Europa |
| U.S.A. .. | | | | | | | | |
| Latinnia .. | 1,000 | | | | | | | |
| Canada .. | 400 | 10 | | | | | | |
| Miscellannia | 800 | 100 | 80 | | | | | |
| Imperia .. | 100 | 300 | 10 | 80 | | | | |
| U.K. .. | 200 | 500 | 500 | 10 | 60 | | | |
| Britannica .. | 400 | 0 | 100 | 200 | 0 | 960 | | |
| Europa .. | 3,300 | 700 | 200 | 30 | 300 | 200 | 500 | |

### Table 3(B): Summary

| Country | Total Bilateral Deficits | Total Bilateral Surpluses | Overall Deficits | Overall Surpluses |
|---|---|---|---|---|
| U.S.A. .. .. | 0 | 6,200 | | 6,200 |
| Latinnia .. | 1,000 | 1,610 | | 610 |
| Canada .. .. | 410 | 890 | | 480 |
| Miscellannia .. | 980 | 320 | 660 | |
| Imperia | 490 | 360 | 130 | |
| U.K. .. .. | 1,270 | 1,160 | 110 | |
| Britannica .. | 1,660 | 500 | 1,160 | |
| Europa .. .. | 5,230 | 0 | 5,230 | |
| | 11,040 | 11,040 | 7,290 | 7,290 |

shown as nil, is of course greater than the total of the overall deficits (or surpluses)—the figure being, from Table 3(B), $m 11,040.

The interesting lesson which can be learned from Table 3 is that though bilateral deficits equivalent to $m 11,040 have to be settled, means of settlement equivalent to only $m 7,290 could suffice, provided (i) that a currency could be used which was freely transferable to, and acceptable to, all countries and could therefore flow freely from the weaker to the stronger countries and (ii) that this currency was available to the five deficit countries in amounts sufficient to cover their respective overall deficits. For let us suppose such an international currency to exist. Then Europa, as the weakest country, would have to provide enough of the international currency to settle all her bilateral deficits—a total of $m 5,230. Britannica, however, whose bilateral deficits total $m 1,660, would have to provide only $m 1,160 since she would in addition pass on the $m 500 received from Europa. Likewise, the U.K., Imperia, and Miscellannia would need to provide the international currency only to the extent of their respective overall deficits, while Canada and Latinnia (and of course the strongest country, the U.S.A.) would not need to provide any of the international currency at all.

The 'saving' of $m 3,750 of the means of settlement ($m 11,040 minus $m 7,290) is the measure of the extent to which, in our example, bilateral deficits could be cleared by 'passing on' currencies received in the same year—instead of 'passing round' currencies, as in the case of circular transfers. It follows that if overall deficits could be settled in currencies which could be both 'passed on' and 'passed round' this could facilitate the clearing not only of the overall deficits themselves but also of all so-called 'compensable' deficits—i.e. of all bilateral deficits in excess of the total of overall deficits. Under such arrangements, all international settlement would proceed on a fully multilateral basis, for no country would mind with whom it ran deficits and with whom surpluses, but would be concerned solely with its overall position.

Unfortunately however a pattern of bilateral deficits which, as in Table 3, calls for a passing on of means of settlement inevitably leads to difficulties which do not arise where deficits can be arranged in closed circuits. That such is the case can best be seen by considering first the strongest country, the U.S.A. in our example. Since the U.S.A. does not have to make any settlements, it has no incentive to accept currencies with the idea of passing them on, except possibly in a later period, when the pattern of bilateral deficits may have changed. The U.S.A. is therefore likely to be somewhat cautious in deciding what currencies she will accept in settlement of her surpluses. Let us suppose that she accepts without limit only her own currency (U.S. dollars) and gold, other currencies being accepted only up to the limits of prearranged 'swings'.[1] If therefore the U.S.A. be assumed to continue for a long period as the strongest country, she will steadily drain the five deficit countries of gold and U.S. dollars, until these became scarce or 'hard'. The evil day may be postponed by dollar gifts and credits, but not indefinitely. Thus there will develop an incentive, beginning probably with Europa but spreading to the other relatively weak countries, to try to settle in a 'softer' medium, and to discriminate in favour of countries which will accept it. For example, Europa may try to persuade Britannica to accept settlements in a 'softer' currency (which the U.S.A. would not accept) by using the argument: 'We cannot pay you in dollars, because we are running short of them, so if you do not accept a softer currency, we shall perforce have to buy less of your goods'. If Europa's policy succeeds against Britannica and other countries, and if these in turn attempt to follow her example, there will develop a 'soft-currency area' wherein settlements are made in currencies not acceptable to the U.S.A. This development will undermine the multilateral basis of settlement, since countries will have an incentive to attempt to run bilateral surpluses with the hard currency countries rather than with the soft currency countries, and to run bilateral deficits with the soft currency countries rather than with the hard currency countries.

If, as we have assumed for purposes of illustration, the U.S.A. will accept certain other countries' currencies up to a limited swing, the hardening of the U.S. dollar may induce the countries enjoying these facilities to restrict the transferability of their currencies. The U.K. might for instance try to stop other countries from settling with the U.S.A. in sterling, since such settlements would use up the accumulation facilities which would otherwise be available to settle the U.K.'s own bilateral

[1]In the real world the United States does not undertake to accumulate the currencies of any other countries.

deficit with the U.S.A. In such circumstances countries holding sterling would have an incentive to prefer to run deficits with the U.K. and with countries to which sterling could be freely transferred, rather than with the U.S.A. Thus here again the multilateral basis of international settlement would be undermined.

In brief, then, the free flow of means of settlement from the weaker to the stronger countries in Table 3 is liable to be interrupted in two ways:

1. in some parts of the world, certain currencies may become too hard for general use in making settlements, and
2. the soft currencies used instead may, since they enjoy at best only limited acceptability in the hard currency area, suffer a restriction of their transferability,

and in either case the multilateral basis of international settlement will be undermined. Moreover, the process which has just been described can be repeated in respect of some other currency, say the Canadian dollar, which would be unlikely to become harder than the U.S. dollar (since no currency could be more acceptable to Canada than one which, like the U.S. dollar, could be used for settling her deficits with both U.S.A. and Latinnia[1]) but might however come to occupy a position somewhere between the U.S. dollar and the soft currencies. There might indeed develop almost as many degrees of hardness as there are currencies, which would eventually lead to a reversion to complete bilateralism.

It must not be concluded from this section that international disequilibria make settlement on a multilateral basis quite impossible, but only that they lead to difficulties whose seriousness depends on the circumstances. It is for instance possible for the currency of a relatively weak country to remain reasonably hard if it is widely believed that she will in due course become much stronger, and the hardness will be further increased if the currency has long enjoyed the status of a world-wide international currency.

[1]Since Latinnia has a deficit only with the U.S.A., there could be no currency more acceptable to her than U.S. dollars.

*The Scope for International Co-operation*

The scope for international co-operation in the field of liquidity is to provide enough means of settlement to accommodate international disequilibria until they either disappear of their own accord, or can be dealt with by any of the means discussed in the next chapter.

If means of settlement can be made available only on a strictly bilateral basis, more will be needed than if settlement can be arranged on a multilateral basis. Apart from this consideration, settlement on a multilateral basis is also desirable in itself, since it enables each country to allow its traders to buy and sell in whichever foreign markets offer the best terms, irrespective of the bilateral deficits and surpluses which ensue.

Settlement on a multilateral basis requires the provision of facilities for clearing compensable bilateral deficits. Such facilities are easy to provide where the bilateral deficits can be arranged in closed circuits: circular offsetting or circular transfers of a national currency are, for example, perfectly suitable in such cases. Where, however, the bilateral deficits cannot be so arranged, the provision of satisfactory clearing arrangements presents much greater difficulties. In this chapter we have explored the difficulties which arise with one particular clearing mechanism, that of transferable currencies. In Chapter IX, dealing with sterling, we shall see how these difficulties show themselves in practice.

The main alternative to transferable currencies as a device for achieving multilateral settlement is some variety of international pooling arrangement, such as the International Monetary Fund or the European Payments Union, whose liquidity provisions will be considered in Chapters VI and VIII respectively.

## CHAPTER IV

# INTERNATIONAL DISEQUILIBRIA

THE feasibility of settling accounts between the different countries of the world depends not only on the availability of suitable means of settlement but also on the size of the accounts which have to be settled. Since in practice the means for international settlement are never indefinitely large, even in cases where accumulation facilities are not subject to a pre-arranged limit, it follows that international liquidity is only a device for accommodating *temporary* deficits; hence in cases of persistent deficits there arises for the deficit countries the problem of how to correct them before their reserves become exhausted. (If their reserves did become exhausted, and still they took no steps to correct their deficits, there would inevitably occur a depreciation of their currencies.)

In this chapter we shall consider the problem of dealing with international disequilibria in the sense of overall deficits and surpluses, and pay little attention to the question of bilateral deficits. This limitation is appropriate because, as we have seen, bilateral deficits and surpluses can easily be cleared provided that all countries can be brought into approximate overall equilibrium.

An individual county, such as Nottinghamshire, is fortunate, not only in having a generous supply of the means of settling her external accounts (due to having a common currency with the other British counties), but also in the fact that an outflow of cash has a strong tendency to be self-correcting. In an independent country, however, the problems arising from the more limited availability of means of settlement are aggravated by the relative inefficiency of the available means for correcting a deficit.

The reasons for the latter can best be seen if we again give rein to our imagination and this time suppose what would happen if Nottinghamshire had its own separate paper currency, the 'Nottspound', and arranged its external payments by adhering to *sterling* as a standard, as Australia does.[1] Let us however assume for the time being that neither Nottinghamshire nor the rest of the United Kingdom has imposed any restrictions on trade, on capital transactions, or on payments, between the two economies. In these hypothetical circumstances, it is clear that despite the absence of any such restrictions, Nottspeople's capital transactions with the rest of Britain would be much less helpful, from the point of view of correcting external disequilibria, than at present.[2] The existence of the two currencies, the Nottspound and the pound sterling, would be a deterrent to investors, whose future profits would be more uncertain if there was a risk that the official exchange rate might eventually be changed or that exchange restrictions might be imposed. Moreover, such borrowing and lending as remained would be considerably distorted by factors which are at present largely absent. Political and social changes affecting only one of the two economies, such as changes in taxation or in industrial regulations, a change of government, a deterioration of industrial relations, or an increase in social unrest, might greatly upset the balance of borrowing and lending between the two economies. Even the fear that such changes might occur would act in the same way. In addition there might be speculative movements of securities, in anticipation of changes in the exchange rate, or panic sales of securities due to fears that exchange controls might be imposed. It is easy to imagine that movements of securities between independent economies, far from being an equilibrating factor, might well be the reverse. Such, at any rate, seems to be the view of most governments, for regulations on international capital movements are almost universal (though in practice they are far from being completely successful in stopping disequilibrating capital movements).

Since Nottspeople's capital transactions with the rest of Britain would probably no longer be equilibrating if the county

[1]Above, p. 33.
[2]Above, p. 16.

achieved monetary independence, we must now pursue the question (which we rather neglected in Chapter I) of whether, and in what circumstances, the county's external *trade* would be equilibrating.

An external deficit due to a falling off in an independent Nottinghamshire's exports to the rest of Britain would be to some extent self-correcting if no steps were taken to offset the depression (and the consequential reduction in imports) due to the decline in exports and also to the resulting decline in the demand for consumption and investment goods.[1] Indeed, the decline in exports might cause an even greater decline in imports, in which case the Nottinghamshire government could, without danger to the county's sterling reserves, take steps to stimulate an appropriate degree of recovery. On the other hand, if the automatic decline in imports proved to be inadequate, the Nottinghamshire government could always take steps to aggravate the depression, for example by requiring a contraction of bank credit.

But curing an external deficit by means of an internal depression is (as we noted in Chapter I) an unpleasant treatment, and we are naturally more interested in the other available remedies. One such remedy might arise merely with the passage of time and the pressure of circumstances, for the depression might well in due course become unnecessary (as a means of dealing with the external deficit) if the effect of the unemployment in Nottinghamshire was to depress the level of wages, and thus to cheapen the prices of Nottinghamshire's goods in relation to goods produced elsewhere. For this outcome would be similar to that of a depreciation of the Nottspound in relation to the pound sterling, which (it will shortly be shown) would in favourable circumstances reduce Nottinghamshire's deficit.

If however a depreciation of the Nottspound could cure the external deficit, why wait for unemployment to act on the level of wages? Workers would obviously resist the reduction of their wages, probably with partial or even complete success, the necessary negotiations would be prolonged and bitter, and unemployment would have to continue until an adequate fall

[1]C.f. above, pp. 15 and 16, and my *Wealth and Income*, Chapter 24.

in the wage level had occurred.[1] Why not instead simply depreciate the Nottspound straight away?

*Devaluation in Favourable Circumstances*

If the Nottspound were reduced in value from one pound sterling to (say) 19 shillings, this would increase the prices in Nottspounds which Nottspeople would have to pay for imported goods. When imported goods became dearer, Nottspeople would buy less of them and consequently need less sterling to pay for them. If, as is likely under free trade, the total expenditure of Nottspeople has been directed in goodly proportion towards imported goods of all kinds, including luxury goods and goods for which passable substitutes can be made locally, and if in addition the diversion of demand from imported to locally produced goods did not greatly bid up the prices of the latter, the reduction in sterling expenditure on imports would be considerable. In technical language we can say that a devaluation of the Nottspound would be particularly efficacious because of Nottinghamshire's high price-elasticity of demand for imports, i.e. because her imports would be choked off rapidly by a rise in their prices.

Let us turn now from Nottinghamshire's imports to her exports. It is likely that under free trade the demand for Nottinghamshire's exports would also be highly price-elastic, partly because Nottinghamshire's customers, like Nottinghamshire herself, would have a high price-elasticity of demand for imports, and partly because a reduction in the sterling prices of Nottinghamshire's exports would enable her to underbid her competitors and thus to supply a higher proportion of her customers' import-requirements. Hence, provided that the increased demand for Nottinghamshire's exports did not greatly bid up their prices in Nottspounds, the effect of devaluation by Nottinghamshire *alone* would be to increase the volume of the county's exports in a much greater proportion than the

[1]The acceptance of this argument against attempting to cure an external deficit by depressing the level of prices does not of course imply that Nottinghamshire should not attempt to prevent her price level from rising. Rising prices would unnecessarily aggravate her deficit and her problem of dealing with it.

reduction in their sterling prices,[1] so that the county's total sterling earnings from her exports would considerably increase.

*Devaluation in Unfavourable Circumstances*

On the assumptions we have made as to the conditions governing Nottinghamshire's demand for imports and supply of exports and those governing the demand for her exports[2] we can conclude that devaluation would be a highly efficient way of improving Nottinghamshire's balance of current payments and thereby correcting her external deficit. Let us now consider how much less efficient devaluation would be if the relevant conditions were otherwise. To start with, let us reverse our previous assumptions as to Nottinghamshire's demand for imports and supply of exports by supposing Nottinghamshire to be (i) liable to suffer from excess demand, (ii) highly inflexible in her economy and (iii) subject to certain kinds of official restrictions. Then, when we have followed through the implications of these possibilities, we can complete the story by reversing our previous assumptions about the demand for Nottinghamshire's exports.

(i) If the level of demand for Nottinghamshire's goods were already so high that output was nearly at its maximum, both the diversion of demand from imported to locally produced goods and the increase in the demand for exports would result in the bidding up of home prices, thereby offsetting the effect of the devaluation. It would then be up to the Nottinghamshire authorities, if they wished the devaluation to be successful in its objective, to eliminate the excess of demand, either by restricting credit, or by increasing taxation, or by some other suitable means. (It would be useless to keep prices down by official controls if excess demand prevented the volume of

[1]If export prices in terms of Nottspounds remained unchanged, they would fall in terms of sterling to the same proportionate extent as the devaluation of the Nottspound in relation to sterling.

[2]We did not make any explicit assumptions as to the conditions governing the supply of Nottinghamshire's imports, because the conditions to be found in practice would almost never be unfavourable to the success of devaluation as a cure for an external deficit. In so far as Nottinghamshire's demand for imports fell off as the result of devaluation, this would tend, if anything, to reduce the sterling prices of imports, never (in any likely circumstances) to increase them.

exports from increasing: such a policy would merely make Nottinghamshire's sterling earnings lower than ever.)

(ii) Unfortunately the avoidance of an excess of *overall* demand for locally produced goods is not a sufficient condition for the avoidance of a serious rise in home prices. Devaluation stimulates the demand for specific types of goods, namely those which are the closest substitutes for imported goods and those which are suitable for export. If the output of these particular types of goods can be increased only with difficulty, and if the home demand for them cannot be much reduced, then a relatively large devaluation will be required to effect a given improvement in the balance of current payments. An increase in the output of the relevant types of goods may well be difficult to achieve if the industries producing them are already operating to the limit of their existing resources of manpower, land, or equipment, since the expansion of output would then require that additional resources of a suitable type should be attracted from other industries—which would be impossible if such resources simply did not exist or if they were located in the wrong place and immobile. A reduction in the home demand for the relevant types of goods would be difficult to achieve if these goods happened to be necessities or, in the case of exportable goods, if the proportion of output sold on the home market was in any case very small.

(iii) If we drop our previous assumption of free trade and imagine that our 'independent' Nottinghamshire follows the almost general present-day practice of independent countries and drastically restricts imports by tariffs, quotas, exchange controls and similar devices, we can no longer argue that there is even the possibility of the county's demand for imports being highly elastic. For if official restrictions have already reduced imports to bare necessities which cannot be produced locally, it would be over-optimistic to expect that devaluation would effect much further reduction.

It may appropriately be noted here that price control and rationing, imposed to hold in check an excessive pressure of home demand, may have the same adverse effect on the elasticity of demand for imports as restrictions imposed specifically on imports. For the inhabitants of an economy suffering from 'suppressed inflation' may be expected to buy the permitted quantities of imported goods, almost irrespectively of the prices charged by the importers. The inhabitants of such an economy will also tend always to buy the permitted quantities of exportable goods, irrespective of their prices, which will make it difficult to expand the volume of exports by diverting supplies from the home market.

Let us now reverse our previous assumption of a highly elastic demand for Nottinghamshire's exports. The lower the elasticity of demand for Nottinghamshire's exports the larger the devaluation needed to achieve a given increase in the county's sterling earnings from her exports. Indeed, below a certain critical elasticity, technically known as the point of 'unit elasticity', Nottinghamshire's sterling earnings would actually fall, the increase in the volume of exports being insufficient to compensate for the reduction in their sterling prices. In such circumstances, it would be best for the Nottinghamshire authorities to tackle an unfavourable balance of current payments not by attempting to stimulate exports by devaluation (or other means), since this would merely represent so much wasted effort, but to concentrate on reducing imports, for example by imposing restrictions on imports or on current payments.

The incentive to impose restrictions, rather than to devalue, would still be present (though not quite so strong) if the demand for Nottinghamshire's exports were of more than unit elasticity, but not much more, that is, if devaluation would have increased Nottinghamshire's sterling earnings but not by very much. For if (to give a hypothetical example) the conditions of export demand were such that a 10 per cent reduction in the sterling prices of Nottinghamshire's exports would cause an increase of only 12 per cent in the quantity bought, and therefore an increase of less than 1 per cent in the total sterling value of Nottinghamshire's exports,[1] it might well be thought that the extra sterling earned by an increase in export production provided an inadequate return for the extra effort involved

[1]If prices change in the ratio of 100 : 90 and quantity bought in the ratio of 100 : 112, total value will change in the ratio of $100 \times 100 : 90 \times 112$ or 100 : 100.8.

—so that it would still be advantageous to deal with an external deficit solely by reducing imports.[1]

The advantage to be gained by resorting to restrictions, rather than to devaluation, when the elasticity of demand for exports is low, is not very great when circumstances are such that imports are rapidly choked off by devaluation, for then a comparatively small devaluation will do the trick and the amount of 'wasted effort' in export production will not be serious. If however imports do not readily respond to devaluation, a low elasticity of demand for exports is a strong argument for preferring restrictions to devaluation.

*Factors Affecting the Elasticity of Demand for Exports*

Let us now abandon our imaginary 'independent' Nottinghamshire and consider as realistically as possible the conditions which determine the elasticity of demand for an economy's exports. The elasticity of demand for our country's exports depends on (i) the elasticity of demand for imports by the various foreign countries which buy our exports, (ii) the importance of the home country as an exporter, compared with rival countries exporting the same kind of goods as we do and (iii) the extent to which our rivals retaliate against a cut in our export prices by cutting theirs too, for instance by following our example and devaluing their currencies.

(i) What might prevent our foreign customers from buying more imports when we reduce our prices, measured in foreign currencies? If our customers do import more, this will tend to *reduce* the demand for the products of their own industries, so that there is no question of their economies being incapable of making the adjustment because of excess demand or of industrial inflexibility. The only serious obstacle which is in practice likely to prevent much increase in our customers' imports is their use of drastic official restrictions on imports.

The widespread use of such restrictions in the modern world can now be seen to be due in part to the operation of a

[1]In technical terms this proposition would be translated thus: Nottinghamshire might consider that the advantage of the greater *volume* of external trade achieved by devaluation would be more than counterbalanced by the simultaneous adverse change in her *terms* of trade (an economy's terms of trade being the ratio of its export prices to its import prices).

vicious circle. For, first, the main reason why countries prefer to deal with external deficits by imposing restrictions on imports rather than by devaluation is that the typical country faces an inelastic demand for its exports. Second, an important reason why the typical country *qua* exporter has this problem is because the typical country *qua* importer has an inelastic demand for imports. Lastly, the main reason why the typical country *qua* importer has an inelastic demand for imports is that it has already imposed so many restrictions on imports.

It is of course true that in a restrictionist world international disequilibria could be corrected by a reduction in the restrictions imposed by the surplus countries rather than by an increase in those imposed by the deficit countries. Unfortunately, however, though deficit countries are sooner or later compelled, by the fear of exhausting their liquidity, to attempt to deal with a persistent disequilibrium, surplus countries are under no such compulsion, and therefore tend in practice to leave on the deficit countries the onus of making the necessary adjustments. Thus if there are no deliberate attempts at international co-operation, there is a constant tendency for restrictions to breed more restrictions, so that instead of each country specializing in those lines of production in which it enjoys the greatest comparative advantage, there is a general drift towards inefficient self-sufficiency.

(ii) We must now take into account the fact that our country may still enjoy a highly elastic demand for exports, even if each of our customers has an inelastic demand for imports, provided that a reduction in our export prices would enable us readily to undercut our rival suppliers in the export markets. This situation would arise only if our country contributes only a small proportion of the world total of exports of each of the commodities she exports. If, for example, our country is an exporter of (let us say) coal, but in small quantities compared with the total coal exports of all countries, a small cut in our export price will probably be sufficient to enable us to undercut our rival exporters to an extent which will represent a large proportionate increase in our export tonnage. We might perhaps double our export tonnage by a (say) 5 per cent reduction in our export price, even if the coal-importing countries had imposed such drastic trade restrictions that the tonnage imported from all sources did not increase at all. If on the other hand our country were the *only* coal exporter, we should have no rival exporters to undercut and a 5 per cent price reduction would decrease our foreign currency earnings unless there followed an increase in total coal imports of over 5 per cent. In general, therefore, countries whose exports are small in amount and widely diversified are likely to experience a much more elastic demand for their exports than are countries whose exports are large in amount and confined to a narrow range of products. It is an unfortunate characteristic of the real world that most countries are either large exporters (like the U.S.A. and Britain) or specialist exporters (like Denmark, Switzerland, Malaya, or Brazil), in consequence of which the elasticity of the demand facing the typical country *qua* exporter is unlikely to be high unless most of the countries of destination have a high elasticity of demand for imports—a condition which is unlikely to be satisfied if the typical country *qua* importer imposes drastic restrictions on trade and payments.

(iii) Even though our country would enjoy a highly elastic demand for her exports if we alone reduced our prices (measured in the importing countries' currencies), we may nevertheless effect little or no increase in our export earnings if the action we take to reduce our prices—in this case currency devaluation—is also taken by our rival exporters. Such retaliation by our competitors is unlikely except where a high proportion of their exports is competitive with ours, but this condition is not infrequently satisfied, at least to some extent, in a world in which most countries are either large exporters or specialist exporters. If for example Britain devalued her currency in an attempt to sell more exports, she would always have to face the possibility that other exporters of manufactures—for instance Belgium and Germany—would follow suit.

Another consideration which is relevant to the elasticity of the demand for our country's exports is the period which is allowed for the adjustment of demand to occur. For example, a 5 per cent cut in our export prices, taking effect as from (say) January, would almost certainly be less effective in increasing the volume of our exports in the following month than in increasing it in the following January, simply because it would take time for the purchasers of our goods in the importing countries to change their trading arrangements so as to take advantage of our lower prices. This delay in the reaction on the part of our customers would be longest if we specialized in the export of finished goods, particularly manufactured articles, rather than of primary commodities. The purchaser of almost any kind of manufactured article tends to be loyal to the brand, or the design, or the producing firm, with which he is already familiar, and in consequence he is not readily induced to transfer quickly his allegiance to another source of supply merely by the quotation of a lower price. For this reason the countries specializing in the export of manufactured articles (Britain, for example) are almost certainly faced with a relatively low short-term elasticity of demand for their exports, and when the other relevant conditions (e.g. the trade restrictions of customer countries) are also such as to make for a low elasticity, then demand in the short term may well be of less than unit elasticity. It is for example probable that a country such as Britain, selling her exports in the restriction-ridden markets of today, would in the short run appreciably reduce, rather than increase, her foreign currency earnings by a reduction in the foreign-currency prices of her exports[1] even though in the longer run earnings would recover and maybe ultimately surpass their original level. (Admittedly, as we shall see in Chapter XI, this argument is not supported by the course of events immediately after the British devaluation in September 1949, when British export earnings *increased*, but this outcome can reasonably be attributed to speculation, which we have not so far taken into account.)

*Summary and Conclusions*

It may be useful to summarize our arguments as to the efficacy of devaluation (and incidentally of other forms of

[1]If Britain allowed sterling to depreciate and thereby brought about a reduction in the foreign-currency prices of British exports, it is conceivable that the short-term reduction in her foreign-currency earnings might be greater than the short-term reduction in her foreign-currency expenditure on imports (induced by the rise in the sterling prices of imports). In this case the short-term effect of depreciation would be not to cure an external deficit but to aggravate it. See above, p. 24.

currency depreciation[1]) by listing as follows the circumstances in which it is unlikely to be preferred to restrictionism as a means for improving a country's balance of current payments.[2]

1. Devaluation has roughly the same effect as import restrictions in circumstances where our supply of exports cannot be increased. Such circumstances may arise (i) through the pressure of excess demand in our home economy or (ii) through the inflexibility of the home economy. Inflexibility is worst where the output of the export industries cannot be increased and where the home demand for exportable goods is either very insistent or already relatively small.
2. Where our supply of exports can be increased without a serious rise in their home-currency prices, devaluation imposes an entirely fruitless burden on our export industries if the demand for our exports has less than unit elasticity and a largely fruitless burden if the elasticity is not much greater than unity. The elasticity of the demand for our exports depends partly on our ability to undercut our competitors, but it is unlikely to be high if other countries do not greatly increase their imports when these become cheaper in terms of their own currencies. The main reason why our customer-countries should not take more imports when they become cheaper is the existence of official restrictions.
3. If the elasticity of demand for our exports is not high, the case for our dealing with our external deficit by resorting to import restrictions in preference to devaluation is strengthened if our own elasticity of demand for imports is low. This will be the case if (i) our competent authorities are unable to prevent the emergence of excess demand or (ii) if our economy is unduly inflexible or (iii) if official restrictions have already reduced our imports to necessities which cannot be produced locally.

[1]The term 'devaluation' is usually reserved for those cases of currency depreciation where, as we have assumed in our examples, the value of the currency is stabilized by official intervention both before and after the depreciation.

[2]It must not be concluded from the foregoing that all arguments for devaluation rest exclusively on its effect on a country's balance of current payments, since it may also be advocated as the only practicable means of stopping 'leaks' in a country's exchange control. See below, Chapters IX and XI.

If circumstances are such that countries prefer to deal with international disequilibria by imposing restrictions rather than by a change of exchange rates, it is preferable that the restrictions imposed by the deficit-countries should be discriminatory, and be designed to reduce their bilateral deficits with the main surplus countries. In so far as deficit countries impose restrictions directed against each other they merely harm each other, without in any way correcting the original disequilibria.[1] It is however unhappily a feature of multilateral means of international settlement (so admirable in other respects) that they provide an incentive for indiscriminate restrictions, since if country A can by means of new restrictions impose a further deficit on B, A will thereby obtain the means of settling part of her own deficit with C, the original surplus country. However, as we have seen, persistent disequilibria tend to undermine the basis of multilateral settlement by leading to the emergence of hard currencies, and this development, in a very rough and ready fashion, calls forth the kind of discrimination that the disequilibrium requires.[2]

It will by now be clear that the scope for international action designed to deal with persistent international disequilibria is very extensive. First, there is the need for agreement to make reciprocal reductions in restrictions on international trade and on international payments, so as to increase the price-elasticity of each country's demand for imports. This reform would not only allow each country to obtain greater benefit from its comparative advantages in different fields of industry but would also restore the efficacy of variations in exchange rates as a means for correcting persistent disequilibria. Second, in so far as restrictions still need to be used for dealing with disequilibria, surplus countries must be persuaded that the correction can be better made by them reducing their restrictions than by deficit countries imposing additional restrictions.

[1]If the deficit countries had chosen to cure their deficits by devaluation and had all devalued by the same percentage, the relative values of their currencies would have remained unchanged, and they would therefore not harm each other.

[2]In this connection, see Professor J. M. Fleming's article 'On Making the Best of Balance of Payments Restrictions on Imports', in the *Economic Journal,* March 1951.

Third, if restrictions do have to be imposed by deficit countries, such countries must be permitted, and indeed encouraged, to direct their restrictions solely against the surplus countries.

*The Concept of 'Suppressed Disequilibrium'*

There remains to be considered an important question of terminology. So far we have described a country as being 'in disequilibrium' only when it has an overall deficit or surplus. We have now to recognize that the same term is sometimes used in a wider sense, to include what might be termed 'suppressed' disequilibria as well as the 'open' disequilibria of overall surpluses and deficits. The notion of a suppressed disequilibrium is based in effect on the acceptance of a distinction between 'satisfactory' and 'unsatisfactory' ways of dealing with an open disequilibrium. If an open disequilibrium is eliminated by a satisfactory means, it is taken to be cured, but if it is eliminated by an unsatisfactory means it is merely 'suppressed'. Unfortunately the criteria by which satisfactory treatments can be distinguished from unsatisfactory ones are rarely made explicit, but the most plausible interpretation of the distinction is that unsatisfactory treatments comprise:

1. an increase in unemployment in the deficit countries, and
2. the imposition by the deficit countries of additional restrictions on international trade[1] or on international payments on current (as distinct from capital) account.

On this basis, satisfactory treatments would include adjustments of exchange rates, a reduction in the restrictions imposed by surplus countries, a tightening up of controls on capital transactions, and finally a curbing of demand in the deficit countries sufficient to stabilize, or even to depress, the prices of their products. (However, a curbing of demand sufficient to depress, and not merely to stabilize, the prices of the deficit countries'

[1]The following excerpt from Article 21, paragraph 6 of the I.T.O. Agreement (see Chapter VII below) illustrates the use of the word 'disequilibrium' to mean 'suppressed disequilibrium':

'If there is a persistent and widespread application of import restrictions under this Article, indicating the existence of a general disequilibrium which is restricting international trade, . . .'

products can perhaps claim to be 'satisfactory' only when prices have actually been reduced to the required extent, for the process of reduction may cause much more social discord and hardship than the other 'satisfactory' treatments.)

Unfortunately the concept of suppressed disequilibria, though useful for theoretical analysis, is difficult to apply in practice. Who shall say, in respect of any country suffering unemployment, how much of its unemployment can be attributed to the need for reducing, or eliminating, an external deficit, and how much is attributable to other factors? Happily this awkward conundrum has not given much trouble in the post-war period, for serious unemployment has been rare.[1] There is also a practical problem in identifying suppressed disequilibrium in the form of restrictions on trade or on current payments, for such restrictions are also used for purposes other than preventing deficits, and it is often difficult to distinguish an unambiguous purpose behind any particular set of restrictions.[2]

[1]See below, Chapter X.

[2]There is however one species of restrictions—namely discriminatory restrictions directed against payments in a particular currency—which is most unlikely to be used for any purpose other than that of closing a deficit. The only other purposes of discriminatory restrictions are political and military, and such cases are readily identifiable.

CHAPTER V

# THE INTERNATIONAL TRANSMISSION OF DEPRESSIONS

DEPRESSIONS may be transmitted from one country to others in the following ways:

1. A certain country, A, develops a business depression, due to a recession of home demand. In consequence A's imports of goods from the rest of the world fall off, and her depression thus spreads spontaneously to other countries.
2. Country A may then attempt to restore her own prosperity by imposing trade or payments restrictions, or depreciating her currency, with the object of diverting home demand from imported to home-produced goods.[1] Since one country's imports are another's exports, such a policy must reduce the level of demand in other countries; hence it is a 'beggar-my-neighbour' remedy for unemployment.[2]

A large reduction in A's imports (whether due to a recession in A's home demand or to A's adoption of beggar-my-neighbour remedies for her unemployment) may undermine not merely her neighbours' prosperity but also their liquidity, for any reduction in A's imports cuts down her neighbours' supply of the means of settling their accounts with A. On the other hand, in so far as A inflicts depression on her neighbours they will normally not wish to import so much from A, which tends to relieve the drain on their means of settling with A. On balance, therefore, the drain of means of settlement to A from her neighbours may not be serious[3]—provided that A's

[1]To simplify the text I have omitted to mention that currency depreciation will affect A's prosperity by affecting exports as well as imports, and that the effect via imports may be unfavourable. See my *Wealth and Income*, Chapter 25.

[2]See Joan Robinson: *Essays in the Theory of Employment*, p. 210.

[3]This is particularly true if A has previously been running an external deficit, or if her neighbours hold substantial reserves of suitable means of settlement.

neighbours take no steps to offset the decline in their prosperity.[1] But if they do attempt to restore their prosperity, and elect to do so by stimulating their home demand (for example by increasing expenditure on public works), this will tend to reverse the decline in their imports from A, and consequently in their payments to A. Thus even if the *immediate* problem which besets A's neighbours is solely that of depression, without serious loss of liquidity, there is still the possibility that the problem of illiquidity may arise when action is under consideration for combating the depression.

As we have seen, the problem of depression may arise among A's neighbours either because of the spontaneous spread of a depression originating in A or because A has adopted beggar-my-neighbour remedies for her unemployment. Beggar-my-neighbour remedies for unemployment are not quite as harmful to other countries as it might at first appear, for in so far as they are successful in restoring prosperity in the country adopting them they will reverse the fall in her imports attributable to the depression (though they will not of course reverse such improvement in her balance of current payments as is due to the imposition of restrictions or to the depreciation of her currency). Nevertheless, beggaring one's neighbours remains reprehensible, even though they are not beggared quite as badly as might at first seem to be the case.

The spontaneous spreading of depression from one country to another raises rather more complicated issues of international morality. What is liable to happen in practice is that the 'victim' countries attempt to insulate themselves by taking steps to cut down their imports more or less in line with the decline in their exports. In this way they hope to balance the reduction in the export demand for their goods by a diversion of internal demand from imported to home-produced goods, thereby restoring their prosperity without however imposing any additional strain on their liquidity. But if A's neighbours react in this way, there will be unfortunate consequences. First, if they reduce their imports by means of additional restrictions and not by currency depreciation, there is a danger (as we have seen) that the restrictions may be imposed without

[1]See above, p. 48.

discrimination against A, in which case the victim countries will quite unnecessarily harm each other. (This would not happen if the victim countries all depreciated their currencies by the same percentage in relation to A's currency, so that the *relative* values of their own currencies remained unchanged.[1]) Second, any restrictions imposed on such an occasion create a permanent vested interest in favour of their indefinite retention, long after the original reason for them has passed away. Third, in so far as the victim countries reduce their imports from A, whether by imposing restrictions or by currency depreciation, this will aggravate A's depression; A may consider this an unfriendly act and attempt to retaliate.

It is difficult to resist the conclusion that A's neighbours should tolerate the import of unemployment and attempt to combat it by an increase, not simply a diversion, of their internal demand; in this way they would alleviate, instead of aggravate, A's misfortune. If, however, they adopted such a policy this would tend to deplete their means of settlement with A. A could of course assist by providing her good neighbours with additional means of settlement, for instance by extending to them additional drawing rights in the form of official grants or loans, but even so the flow of settlements to A from her neighbours could not go on indefinitely. What therefore A's neighbours would have to demand of A, in return for their adoption of a policy of stimulating the level of internal demand in their own economies, is that A in turn should make prompt and strenuous efforts to stimulate her own internal demand, and thereby deal effectively with the root cause of all the trouble.

The scope for co-ordinated international action against business depressions is thus seen to be extensive. The following list of possibilities is derived mainly from two recent international reports on the subject of unemployment[2]:

[1]See footnote 1 on p. 58.

[2]*National and International Measures for Full Employment*, a report presented in 1949 by a group of experts to the Secretary-General of the United Nations, and

*Action against Unemployment*, a study published in 1950 by the International Labour Office.

The detailed recommendations of these reports are well worthy of study but must be regarded as controversial.

1. There should be agreement to outlaw beggar-my-neighbour remedies for unemployment.
2. Each country should announce in advance domestic measures which would come into operation at the onset of a depression, stating in addition what criterion would be taken to indicate the onset of a depression.
3. International arrangements should be made to restore the liquidity of victim countries.
4. Reassured by these arrangements, countries which fear the possibility of contagion from external depression might be both able and willing to forgo the practice of insulation.
5. Lastly, there might be international action to assist the depressed country in taking measures to stimulate her internal demand.[1]

It may be wondered why, with such widespread concern at the phenomenon of the international transmission of depressions, there should be so little interest in the contrary phenomenon of the international transmission of inflation, for an inflation in one country spreads to its neighbours in exactly the same way as a depression.[2] This relative lack of interest can be attributed to the following factors. First, in the past depression has been commoner than inflation, and in a situation where most countries are depressed the occurrence of inflation in one country, or several countries, is beneficial to the rest of the world. Only in a situation of world-wide full employment (whether of labour or of productive capacity) is inflation in one country a cause for misgivings among its neighbours. Such situations have occurred only infrequently in the past. Second, if a country is experiencing an inflation, the rest of the world gains, rather than loses, in liquidity, so here again there is no cause for complaint. It is the inflating country which loses liquidity, and such a country is thus given an added incentive to restrain its inflation or alternatively is forced itself to insulate its economy from neighbouring economies. Hence it follows that it is the inflating country which has to bear most of the burden of readjustment, and in consequence the neighbouring

[1]See *Action against Unemployment*, Chapter VIII.

[2]The I.M.F. has been greatly concerned with problems of inflation (see Chapter VI) but in another context, namely as a cause of external disequilibria.

countries are less concerned than they would be if it were a case of depression.

Nevertheless, it may be that too little attention has been paid to the international propagation of inflation. With so many governments committed, not only to full employment policies as such, but also to ambitious social and defence policies whose net effect is inevitably to increase demand, it may well be that in the future (as in the immediate post-war years) the problem of inflation will be at least as serious as that of depression. What may happen in these circumstances is that countries may fight inflation at home by taking steps (e.g. currency appreciation or restrictions on exports) aimed at reducing exports, stimulating imports, or a combination of both, so as to provide their home market with more goods on which their excessive home demand can expend itself. Examples of such policies are to be found in the post-war period,[1] and though they have usually been kept in check by the need to prevent an excessive loss of liquidity, they could in conceivable circumstances prove a serious embarrassment to neighbours who were also struggling to combat inflation in their own economies.

The need for developing international rules of the game to check the 'export' of inflation will become more pressing in so far as means are introduced to increase international liquidity. For then the task of insulating the 'inflating' economy from the rest of the world will not be imposed so forcibly as at present on the inflating economy itself, and may therefore need to be tackled also by the victim countries, preferably acting in close collaboration both with the inflating country and with each other. It thus seems possible that the future may require that international measures to combat depression should be adaptable to deal with the opposite malady of inflation.

[1]See below, p. 151.

# *PART TWO*

# *THE MACHINERY OF INTERNATIONAL MONETARY CO-OPERATION*

## CHAPTER VI

## THE INTERNATIONAL MONETARY FUND

THE I.M.F. Agreement is much the most comprehensive international monetary convention ever to be agreed on a world-wide basis, and the I.M.F. itself is much more ambitious in its objectives than any other international monetary institution. In this chapter and the next, the Fund will be examined with special regard to each of the different fields which have already been noted as offering scope for international co-operation.

The Fund Agreement,[1] which provided for the setting up of the Fund and for its *modus operandi*, was one of two drafted at Bretton Woods in July 1944, the other agreement being concerned with the Fund's sister institution, the International Bank for Reconstruction and Development. The Fund Agreement had already been foreshadowed by the publication in 1943 of the British Keynes Plan[2] and the American White Plan.[3] Neither of these plans was nearly as detailed and comprehensive as the Fund Agreement, but the Keynes Plan made certain proposals, concerning the provision of additional liquidity, which went much beyond the provisions of the Agreement and which will require special mention.

The Fund commenced operations in March 1947, a few

[1] *United Nations Monetary and Financial Conference, held at Bretton Woods*. Cmd. 6546, 1944.

[2] *Proposals for an International Clearing Union*, Cmd. 6437, 1943.

[3] *United States Proposal for a United and Associated Nations Stabilization Fund*, reprinted by H.M.S.O., 1943.

months later than the Bank. The present membership is very extensive, the chief non-members being the U.S.S.R., the European 'Peoples' Democracies' (though Czechoslovakia has remained a member), the former European neutrals (except Sweden), Germany, Japan, New Zealand and Argentina. A list of the members is given in Table 4 on page 69.

*The Objects of the Fund*

The Fund is required by its charter, the Fund Agreement, to appear in two roles, corresponding very roughly to those of a banker and of an umpire. In its former role the Fund engages in transactions with its members for the purpose of supplying them with additional means of international settlement, in broadly the same way that a banker grants advances to his customers, though we must beware of pressing this analogy too far. In its latter role the Fund is required by its charter to administer and enforce certain 'rules of the game' laid down in the charter itself for the regulation of international monetary affairs. These 'rules of the game' are partly aimed at facilitating the work of the Fund *qua* banker, but their main purpose is undoubtedly to further certain basic objectives to which the signatories of the Agreement are committed. These objectives are in brief: 'to facilitate the expansion and balanced growth of international trade, and to contribute thereby to the promotion and maintenance of high levels of employment and real income', 'to promote exchange stability, to maintain orderly exchange arrangements among members, and to avoid competitive exchange depreciation', 'to assist in the establishment of a multilateral system of payments in respect of current transactions between members and in the elimination of foreign exchange restrictions which hamper the growth of world trade', and 'to shorten the duration and lessen the degree of disequilibrium in the international balances of payments of members'.[1]

In this chapter and the next we shall consider the work of the Fund in furtherance of its various objectives, but under headings which are based more closely on the argument of Part One of this book than on the phraseology of the Fund

[1]The quotations are from Article 1 of the Fund Agreement.

## TABLE 4

LIST OF MEMBERS OF THE I.M.F. IN OCTOBER 1951, WITH THEIR RESPECTIVE QUOTAS[1]

*(expressed in millions of U.S. dollars)*

| *Member* | *Quota* | *Member* | *Quota* |
|---|---|---|---|
| Australia | 200 | Iran | 35 |
| Austria | 50 | Iraq | 8 |
| Belgium | 225 | Italy | 180 |
| Bolivia | 10 | Lebanon | 4.5 |
| Brazil | 150 | Luxemburg | 10 |
| Canada | 300 | Mexico | 90 |
| Ceylon | 15 | Netherlands | 275 |
| Chile | 50 | Nicaragua | 2 |
| China | 550 | Norway | 50 |
| Colombia | 50 | Pakistan | 100 |
| Costa Rica | 5 | Panama | 0.5 |
| Cuba | 50 | Paraguay | 3.5 |
| Czechoslovakia | 125 | Peru | 25 |
| Denmark | 68 | Philippines | 15 |
| Dominican Republic | 5 | Sweden | 100 |
| Ecuador | 5 | Syria | 6.5 |
| Egypt | 60 | Thailand | 12.5 |
| El Salvador | 2.5 | Turkey | 43 |
| Ethiopia | 6 | Union of South Africa | 100 |
| Finland | 38 | United Kingdom | 1,300 |
| France | 525 | United States | 2,750 |
| Greece | 40 | Uruguay | 15 |
| Guatemala | 5 | Venezuela | 15 |
| Honduras | 0.5 | Yugoslavia | 60 |
| Iceland | 1 | | |
| India | 400 | TOTAL | 8,136.5 |

Agreement. The headings which we shall use are: 'Exchange Rates', 'Additional Liquidity' (dealing with the Fund *qua* banker), 'Multilateral Settlement', 'Restrictions on Trade and Payments', 'The Treatment of Disequilibria' and 'The International Transmission of Depressions'.

[1]Quotas are explained below, p. 75.

*Exchange Rates*

As we have seen, one of the purposes of the Fund is 'to promote exchange stability, to maintain orderly exchange arrangements among members, and to avoid competitive exchange depreciation', and Article IV of the Agreement seeks to attain this end by requiring members to agree with the Fund suitable gold par values for their respective currencies, so as to create a system of stable exchange rates with orderly cross rates. The gold par values thus agreed must be observed in all transactions involving the exchange of one member's currency against another's or against gold. Only countries which have agreed par values with the Fund may have access to the Fund's resources, and any but small changes in the par values agreed require the Fund's approval. At present there are only seven members—Austria, Ceylon, China, Greece, Italy, Turkey and Uruguay—for whom par values have never been agreed and three—Peru, France and Canada—whose official parities have lapsed.[1] In many of these cases, however, the lack of official parities has not prevented a considerable degree of *de facto* stability of exchange rates. On the other hand, as we shall see, there is a number of member countries which, though having an agreed parity, nevertheless also allow non-parity rates as part of their multiple currency practices. Moreover, though the Fund has consistently 'deprecated international transactions in gold at premium prices',[2] its efforts in this direction have been largely unavailing whenever private hoarders have been prepared to pay premium prices, as was the case in 1950–1.[3]

The Fund does not take 'stability' to mean 'rigidity' of exchange rates, and (as we shall see below) is prepared to admit changes in par values as a means for curing persistent international disequilibria. In particular, the Fund approved of the widespread devaluations of September 1949.

'The Fund attaches great importance to the maintenance

[1]France's par value lapsed in January 1948, when she introduced disorderly cross rates (see below, p. 71). Canada's par value lapsed in September 1950 (see p. 172). Peru's par value lapsed in November 1949.

[2]I.M.F.'s *Annual Report*, 1950, p. 70.

[3]*Economist*, 17.2.51, p. 388.

of orderly cross rates',[1] on the grounds that disorderly cross rates must distort trade relationships in circumstances in which trade and payments are not already completely bilateral. If, for example, the official sterling-dollar rate ruling in Britain and the United States is £1=$4, but the lira-sterling and lira-dollar direct rates are such that the sterling-dollar cross rate in Italy is £1=$2.60[2], then goods will be encouraged to flow from the Sterling Area to Italy and from Italy to America in preference to going from the Sterling Area direct to America, irrespective of the real merits of such roundabout trade.[3] 'Export and import restrictions may limit the scope of such transactions, but it will be difficult to check them entirely when the goods diverted are raw materials which can be converted into manufactured goods for which the United States offers a market.'[4] In addition to any 'real' losses resulting from diverting trade unnecessarily into a roundabout course, there is the serious consequence that the victim of the disorderly cross rate (the Sterling Area in this example) earns lire, a currency unacceptable for settlements with the United States, instead of U.S. dollars. Naturally the victims share the Fund's dislike of disorderly cross rates, and in particular, Britain disliked the disorderly sterling-dollar cross rates which prevailed in Italy prior to November 1948 and in France between January 1948 and October 1949, as the result of these countries each allowing a free market in dollars. Happily in these two cases the disputes were settled amicably: Italy agreed in November

[1]*Annual Report*, 1949, p. 22.

[2]This example is taken from an address by M. Gutt at Harvard on 13th February, 1948, entitled 'The Practical Problem of Exchange Rates'. M. Gutt was then the Chairman of the Executive Board of the Fund.

[3]Suppose for the sake of argument that the direct exchange rates between the lira and the $ and £ are respectively $1=600 lire and £1=1,560 lire, giving a sterling-dollar cross rate of £1=2.6, as in M. Gutt's example, compared with a direct sterling-dollar rate of £1= $4. Now suppose further that the sterling cost price in England of a certain consignment of Sterling Area produce is £1,000. The equivalent dollar cost, if the consignment were sent direct to the United States, would be $4,000. If however the consignment were sent to Italy the equivalent lira cost would be 1,560,000 lire, and if the consignment were then re-exported to the United States its equivalent dollar cost would be only $2,600. Thus the roundabout shipment of the consignment would save the American purchaser $1,400, less the extra transport costs and the charges of the extra middlemen.

[4]*Annual Report*, 1948, p. 27.

1948 that the official lira-sterling rate should be henceforth determined by applying the direct sterling-dollar rate to the free lira-dollar rate, while France made important concessions to the British viewpoint at about the same time[1] and in the following year, soon after sterling was devalued, went over entirely to the Italian procedure.

The timing of the final French concession is significant, since it illuminates one of the motives for allowing disorderly cross rates. For both France and Italy had argued that the harm they were doing Britain in allowing a disorderly sterling-dollar cross rate was mainly a means of compensating for the harm Britain was doing them in fixing an 'unfair' direct sterling-dollar rate. Britain, they argued in effect, had agreed with the I.M.F. an excessively high par value which produced an official direct rate of £1=$4, whereas the 'fair' value of the £ was considerably lower, say £1=$3 or thereabouts. The alleged unfairness of the rate of £1=$4 arose in part from the fact that British importer with £1 to spend was (at this rate of exchange) no less attractive a customer to a French or Italian exporter than an American importer with $4 to spend, whereas the French and Italian authorities (who wanted their exporters to sell to the United States and earn dollars) would have preferred that £1 should be considerably less attractive than $4. If the £ had been worth only (say) $3, France and Italy would have obtained their 'fair' share of the American market. The other aspect of the alleged over-valuation of sterling in relation to the dollar was that it made British goods too expensive in relation to American goods, which gave French and Italian importers an inconvenient bias towards buying from the United States.

There seems to be no satisfactory way of striking a balance of blame as between the countries concerned. On the one hand both France and Italy could argue that, though short of dollars, they were continuously accumulating sterling. On the other

[1]After October 1948 the sterling-franc rate applicable to trade transactions was calculated by applying the direct sterling-dollar rate to the effective franc-dollar rate for trade transactions (this rate being the mean of the official and free franc-dollar rates). Thus between October 1948 and September 1949 the disorderly sterling-dollar cross rate in Paris applied only to non-trade transactions.

hand Britain could argue that a devaluation of sterling would prove a mixed blessing to France and Italy, since it would increase Britain's competitive power in export markets,[1] and that if France and Italy were embarrassed by their sterling they should reduce their restrictions on imports from Britain. Happily these conflicting arguments did not lead to a prolonged deadlock, though in the case of France the final solution was reached only after the devaluation of sterling.

Other cases of disorderly cross rates have occurred in the post-war period, but none comparable in seriousness to the two we have already considered. There are, however, cases where disorderly cross rates, or arrangements very similar thereto, have arisen by virtue of the use of multiple exchange rates, a device which we must now consider.

Much of the largest gap now remaining in the orderliness of exchange rates is the continued prevalence of multiple exchange rates. Under Article VIII, Section 3 of the Fund Agreement, 'No member shall engage in . . . any discriminatory currency arrangements or multiple currency practices' without the approval of the Fund, subject to certain relaxations under Article XIV in the 'transitional period'. However in its *First Annual Report on Exchange Restrictions*, dated 1st March, 1950, the Fund noted no important reduction in this particular type of restriction, which has for a long time found particular favour in South America.

To a large extent the Fund's attitude to multiple currencies is simply part of its general hostility to payments restrictions of all kinds, but in its official statement in 1947 on *Multiple Currency Practices*[2] there is a sentence which suggests that such practices are regarded with less favour (or more disfavour) than quantitative restrictions, for,

> Whenever it is inconvenient to deal with both . . . simultaneously, priority should be given to those features which affect

[1]It was indeed for this reason that France complained in September 1949 that the devaluation of sterling was excessive. See footnote 1, p. 171. It may be noted that neither France nor Italy suggested that the alleged over-valuation of sterling increased their *overall* deficits, and the presumption is of course that it would tend to reduce them.

[2]Reproduced in *First Annual Report on Exchange Restrictions*, p. 140.

exchange stability and orderly exchange arrangements among members.

One reason for the Fund's attitude on this matter is the fact (which we have already noted) that multiple currency practices can take forms which amount in effect to disorderly cross rates. Thus we are informed that the Fund has also worked 'to eliminate the more objectionable features of multiple rate systems, such as discrimination between countries of destination or of origin'.[1] On the other hand, it may perhaps be inferred that in the Fund's view multiple currency practices may be the most readily workable type of currency restriction in a country lacking a bureaucracy adequate in size and efficiency, since the licensing of individual transactions represents a heavy administrative burden and can readily lead to widespread corruption. Multiple currency practices also have the advantage that the monopolistic profits arising from the restrictions go to the state, not to private traders who handle the imported goods.[2] In the words of one of the Fund's reports, 'certain countries, particularly in Latin America, have used them [multiple currency practices] as a means of restricting imports without resort to complicated administrative machinery and without giving the recipients of import licences oppor-

[1]*Annual Report*, 1949, p. 24. Multiple selling rates may discriminate either according to the categories of transactions for which the foreign currency is required (e.g. foreign currencies may be sold more dearly for luxury goods than for necessities) or according to the country to which the payment is to be made (e.g. payments to the United States may be penalized by making U.S. dollars very dear). The latter type of discrimination inevitably corresponds very closely with a disorderly cross rate. Multiple buying rates can likewise discriminate either according to the type of transaction or according to the country from which the foreign currency has been obtained.

[2]Restrictions on trade and payments may be either *quantitative* restrictions (where certain kinds of transactions are prohibited except under licence) or *cost* restrictions (where the restrictions merely affect the cost of a commodity or currency). In the former case the traders who are fortunate enough to obtain licences cannot easily be prevented from exploiting for their own profit the scarcities which result from the restrictions. In the latter case traders cannot exploit the situation, since everybody who is prepared to pay the official levy (whether it be e.g. an import duty or an 'unfavourable' exchange rate) is quite free to trade, and traders' profits are thus kept down to the competitive rate.

tunities for large windfall profits. They have also had fiscal significance in some countries. . . .'[1]

*Additional Liquidity*

The Fund offers new facilities to its members for additional liquidity. These facilities are arranged thus: under Article III it is provided that each member shall have a *quota*,[2] and must make a subscription to the Fund, partly in gold but mainly in its domestic currency, equal in value to its quota. For this purpose, all currencies are valued at their official gold par values, as determined under Article IV. In return, members are afforded purchase rights against the pool of currencies thus formed. These purchase rights are multilateral (a member can purchase whichever currency it needs) but are limited and conditional.

The limitation clause, which is Article V, Section 3 (*a*) (iii), gives a member access to the Fund's resources only if

> The proposed purchase would not cause the Fund's holdings of the purchasing member's currency to increase by more than 25 per cent of its quota during the period of twelve months ending on the date of the purchase nor to exceed 200 per cent of its quota, but the 25 per cent limitation shall apply only to the extent that the Fund's holdings of the member's currency have been brought above 75 per cent of its quota if they had been below that amount.

This clause is subject to a waiver clause, Article V, Section 4, giving the Fund discretionary power to waive the limitation, 'especially in the case of members with a record of avoiding large or continuous use of the Fund's resources'.

The I.M.F. Agreement, in its liquidity provisions, follows more closely the White Plan than the Keynes Plan, which suggested different machinery and proposed a much greater amount of additional means of settlement. The Keynes Plan gave the international body, which was to be called the 'Currency Union', the authority to create an entirely new paper currency, *bancor*, which all members would undertake to

[1] *Annual Report*, 1948, p. 27.
[2] See Table 4, p. 69.

accept as a means of settlement and against which each member had a limited overdraft right. The overdraft rights enjoyed by the various countries would however have been much greater in amount than the purchase rights they enjoy as members of the Fund. Thus as a member of the Fund, the United Kingdom's quota is $1.3 billions, so that under the limitation clause the United Kingdom can at best get an increase in liquidity of that amount, spread over four years. Under the Keynes Plan, however, the United Kingdom would have enjoyed an initial quota of more than $4 billions, which by now would have increased to about $10 billions, and three-quarters of the quota would have represented an overdraft facility.[1] Another, and even more important, difference between the Keynes Scheme and the I.M.F. is that under the latter the maximum contribution that a surplus country can be called upon to make is its total initial subscription (equal to its quota), whereas the Keynes Scheme required a surplus country to accept bancor from all deficit countries up to the limit of their aggregate overdraft facilities. Admittedly the comparatively limited facilities of the Fund are supplemented by those of the International Bank, but the Bank's resources are available solely to provide members with foreign currency requirements for specific investment projects, not to provide 'free' (i.e. unhypothecated) liquidity.[2]

The Keynes Plan and the I.M.F. also differ very considerably as regards the conditions on which members are eligible to exercise their drawing rights. Under the former scheme, the only conditions attaching to a member country's use of overdraft rights up to three quarters of its quota are set out in paragraph (8) (*b*) of the White Paper, as follows:

> The Governing Board may require from a member State having a debit balance reaching a *half* of its quota the deposit of suitable collateral against its debit balance. Such collateral shall,

[1]The figures are based on the quota formula in paragraph (5) of Cmd. 6437, and on the overdraft rights as set out in paragraph (8). The increase in the U.K.'s quota would have occurred since the Keynesian quotas were to be varied on the basis of changes in the value of each country's foreign trade.

[2]Cf. the statement of Mr. J. Burke Knapp, representative of the Bank, to the United Nations Economic and Social Council, 12th July, 1950.

at the discretion of the Governing Board, take the form of gold, foreign or domestic currency or Government bonds, within the capacity of the member State. As a condition of allowing a member State to increase its debit balance to a figure in excess of a half of its quota, the Governing Board may require all or any of the following measures:—

(i) a stated reduction in the value of the member's currency, if it deems that to be the suitable remedy;

(ii) the control of outward capital transactions if not already in force; and

(iii) the outright surrender of a suitable proportion of any separate gold or other liquid reserve in reduction of its debit balance.

Furthermore, the Governing Board may recommend to the Government of the member State any internal measures affecting its domestic economy which may appear to be appropriate to restore the equilibrium of its international balance.

These are clearly conditions which any member country could fulfil if it wished to, so that in spite of them the drawing rights remain irrevocable or automatic. This is far from being the case with the Fund, whose members are specifically denied access to the Fund's resources either 'to meet a large or sustained outflow of capital'[1] or again if they make an unauthorized change in their par values,[2] and are in addition subject to the wide prohibitions of Article V, Section 3(*a*) (i), Article V, Section 5, Article XV, Section 2(*a*), and Article XX, Section 4(*i*).[3] Taken together, these provisions mean first, that the Fund's resources are intended for financing only current, and not capital, transactions (even though, as we shall see in Chapter IX, it is sometimes virtually impossible in practice to prevent the latter from being disguised as the former), and second that certain other *transactions* are ineligible and certain *members* are ineligible, the criterion of ineligibility in both cases being left very largely to the Fund's own judgment.

The Fund has in practice interpreted these 'ineligibility provisions' in the light of the fact that, with its limited resources,

[1]Article VI, Section 1.

[2]Article IV, Section 6.

[3]An additional complication is the Scarce Currency Clause (Article VII), which will be considered later on.

it can enjoy a continuous useful existence only if countries exercising purchase rights in due course restore the *status quo* by repurchasing their own currencies from the Fund. It therefore follows that the main purpose of the Fund's resources is to provide 'temporary' assistance: 'Authority to use the resources of the Fund is limited to use in accordance with its purposes to give temporary assistance in financing balance of payments deficits on current account.'[1] Now the Agreement itself, in Article V, Section 7, specifies certain circumstances in which a member country must use its own monetary reserves[2] for repurchasing its own currency from the Fund, but the circumstances laid down[3] do not help the Fund to decide in advance whether a given disequilibrium is going to be temporary. Thus the Fund is left to decide on the basis of its own judgment, and its task is liable to be difficult and even delicate.

In some cases no doubt, a disequilibrium could be judged temporary simply on the ground that it would correct itself, without any official action being required by the country concerned. Thus, for instance, a country might require abnormally large imports in a particular year, due to having an exceptionally bad harvest: this would give rise to a disequilibrium lasting for one year and no longer. In other cases, however, a disequilibrium could be expected to be temporary only if the authorities in the countries concerned seemed able and willing to take effective remedial action. In such cases the Fund would have to decide first, what kind of remedial action, if any, was possible, and second, whether the authorities in the country concerned could be trusted to carry it out.

In fact the Fund has adopted a highly cautious attitude:

> The Executive Board recognized that in starting operations in a war-devastated world before relief and reconstruction

[1]From a declaration of the Fund on 26th September, 1946.

[2]A country's 'monetary reserves' correspond, in the terminology of Chapter III, to the official net holding of international assets, except that inconvertible currencies are excluded. For a precise definition, see Article XIX.

[3]The purpose of the repurchase provisions of the Fund Agreement is solely to ensure that 'members will not use the resources of the Fund, directly or indirectly, to build up their independent monetary reserves' (*Annual Report*, 1949, p. 46). In fact very few repurchases have occurred.

> requirements had been fully met, the Fund was running the risk that some of its resources might be used for other than temporary assistance and this was pointed out in the first Annual Report of the Executive Directors. It was thought desirable to assume this risk in order that the Fund might make a contribution to the maintenance of national economies and of exchange stability during the transitional period.
>
> In considering applications for the use of the Fund's resources during this period, the Executive Board has endeavoured to limit the risk involved to a minimum.
>
> . . . The Fund has emphasized to members that the purpose of the use of the Fund's resources is to give them time to make necessary readjustment and not to avoid the necessity of such readjustments.[1]

In particular, the Fund took the view that countries receiving Marshall Aid should request the purchase of U.S. dollars from the Fund only in exceptional or unforeseen cases.[2] In consequence of this caution, the Fund's resources of gold and U.S. dollars (the only means of settlement acceptable to the United States) have been used only to the extent of about one quarter, despite the world-wide dollar shortage prior to 1950, while only negligible quantities of other currencies have been bought. The details of the Fund's transactions are given below in Table 5. The obvious, and almost certainly correct, interpretation of these figures is that in the Fund's view the post-war disequilibria have so far been only to a minor extent of a temporary character.

### *Multilateral Settlement*

One of the purposes of the Fund is 'to assist in the establishment of a *multilateral* system of payments in respect of current transactions between members . . ',[3] but apart from the multilateral character of members' purchase rights (and these, we have seen, are limited and only conditionally available), the Agreement seems to have laid down an end without explicitly prescribing the means.

The Agreement does not prescribe the use of any specific

[1] *Annual Report*, 1948, pp. 46 and 47.
[2] *Annual Report*, 1949, p. 43.
[3] Article I. My italics.

## TABLE 5

PURCHASES OF CURRENCIES FROM THE I.M.F.
UP TO 31ST JANUARY, 1951

(*All figures are expressed in millions of U.S. dollars*)

| Country exercising Purchase Rights | Purchases $ million |
|---|---|
| United Kingdom | 300 |
| France | 125 |
| India | 100 |
| Netherlands | 75 |
| Brazil | 65 |
| Belgium | 33[1] |
| Mexico | 22 |
| Australia | 20 |
| Norway | 16 |
| Denmark | 10 |
| South Africa | 10 |
| Others | 35[2] |
| TOTAL | 811 |

| *Currencies Purchased* | *$ million* |
|---|---|
| U.S. dollars | 766 |
| Sterling | 34 |
| Belgian francs | 11 |
| TOTAL | 811 |

international currency. Gold has operational significance in the Fund as a common denominator in which currency values

[1]Of which $21 millions have been repurchased; i.e. Belgium bought back for 21 million dollars some of the Belgian francs previously paid to the Fund in exchange for 33 million dollars.

[2]Of which $10 millions have been repurchased.

are expressed, but its use as a means of payment is left largely to the discretion of the individual members.[1] No new international currency is to be created. Nor is any express provision made for the use of a national currency, such as sterling, as an international currency. To the layman it might seem that the clause directed against exchange restrictions may be intended to make *all* currencies potential international currencies by prohibiting all restrictions on 'transfers' as well as on 'payments' for current transactions.[2] Apparently however the legal interpretation of 'transfers' in this clause does not require a member country to make its currency transferable in the sense in which we have been using the term, i.e. transferable as between one foreigner and another.

If Members are not committed, but only permitted, by the Fund Agreement to make their currencies transferable in our sense of the term, the only remaining way in which the Agreement might be claimed to provide for multilateral settlement is by virtue of the so-called 'repatriation clause', Article VIII, Section 4(*a*), which requires that, subject to various exceptions set out in 4(*b*):

> Each member shall buy balances of its currency held by another member if the latter, in requesting the purchase, represents—
>
> (i) that the balances to be bought have been recently acquired as a result of current transactions; or
>
> (ii) that their conversion is needed for making payments for current transactions.
>
> The buying member shall have the option to pay either in the currency of the member making the request or in gold.

But one of the exceptions listed in Section 4(*b*) exempts from the repatriation obligation any member

[1]However, as we saw above, the *price* of gold is not left to the discretion of the individual members.

[2]The clause in question, Article VIII, Section 2(*a*), states that (subject to the Scarce Currency Clause and the clause governing transitional arrangements, both of which we shall consider below):

> . . . no member shall, without the approval of the Fund, impose restrictions on the making of payments and transfers for current international transactions.

> . . . for any reason not entitled to buy currencies of other members from the Fund for its own currency,

so that no member need repatriate his currency unless he is eligible to exercise purchase rights against the Fund. Thus we are back to our original conclusion that the I.M.F. Agreement explicitly provides for multilateral settlement only in so far as members can use their purchase rights, which are limited in amount and only conditionally available.

It would therefore seem that in practice the Fund must rely, for the achievement of its aim of settlement on a multilateral basis, on some currency (whether gold or a national currency like U.S. dollars or sterling) achieving wide acceptability as a means of international settlement, or alternatively on the development of several international currencies all freely exchangeable one against the other at stable exchange rates. So far the currencies which *prima facie* best satisfy the Fund's requirements are gold and U.S. dollars, both of which are widely acceptable and freely transferable and which moreover have the advantage of being freely exchangeable one against the other (at the official parity of $35=1 fine ounce) at the United States Treasury. However, the excessive hardness of the U.S. dollar, and therefore of gold, at any rate up to the end of 1949, has operated against their general use as international currencies.[1] The other important candidate for the role of international currency is sterling, where the main weakness is its restricted transferability and its inconvertibility into gold and dollars. However, despite these defects, sterling enjoys immense popularity as an international currency, as we shall see in Chapter IX.[2]

[1]See Chapter X.

[2]The Fund is not unappreciative of the extent to which the attainment of its objective of multilateral liquidity hinges on the development of international currencies, particularly the U.S. dollar and sterling. See e.g. *Annual Report*, 1947, p. 37.

CHAPTER VII

# THE INTERNATIONAL MONETARY FUND
## (*Continued*)

### *Restrictions on Trade and Payments*

ONE of the purposes of the Fund is to assist 'in the elimination of foreign exchange restrictions which hamper the growth of world trade'.[1] To this end, Article VIII, Section 2(*a*), which has already been mentioned, provides that:

> Subject to the provisions of Article VII, Section 3(*b*), and Article XIV, Section 2, no member shall, without the approval of the Fund, impose restrictions on the making of payments and transfers for current international transactions.

Of the two exceptions mentioned in this quotation, the former is the Scarce Currency Clause, to be considered below, and the latter, referring to arrangements in the transitional period, includes the following provision:

> In the post-war transitional period members may, notwithstanding the provisions of any other articles of this Agreement, maintain and adapt to changing circumstances (and, in the case of members whose territories have been occupied by the enemy, introduce where necessary) restrictions on payments and transfers for current international transactions. Members shall, however, have continuous regard in their foreign exchange policies to the purposes of the Fund. . . . In particular, members shall withdraw restrictions maintained or imposed under this Section as soon as they are satisfied that they will be able, in the absence of such restrictions, to settle their balance of payments in a manner which will not unduly encumber their access to the resources of the Fund.

Under Section 4 of the same Article the end of the transi-

[1]From Article I (iv).

tional period is set conditionally at 'five years after the date on which the Fund begins operations', which in practice will be April 1952. After that date any member still retaining any restrictions inconsistent with the full obligations of membership,

> . . . shall consult the Fund as to their further retention. The Fund may, if it deems such action necessary in exceptional circumstances, make representations to any member that conditions are favorable for the withdrawal of any particular restriction, or for the general abandonment of restrictions, inconsistent with the provisions of any other articles of this Agreement. The member shall be given a suitable time to reply to such representations. If the Fund finds that the member persists in maintaining restrictions which are inconsistent with the purposes of the Fund . . . [the Fund] may declare the member ineligible to use the resources of the Fund.[1]

Thus the full obligation to avoid exchange restrictions is relaxed at any rate until 1952, but members are nevertheless required in the meantime to progress as far as possible in the right direction. The Fund, since its inception, has constantly reminded its members 'that the transitional period should not be protracted indefinitely, but provide the time necessary to overcome obstacles to the elimination of restrictions'.[2] In particular, the Fund has attempted to secure the removal of exchange restrictions 'not primarily motivated by balance of payments considerations',[3] but intended rather to protect home industries, to raise revenue for the government, or to achieve still other objectives. The chief attraction of protection, when it is not (as it so often is) simply a device for benefiting a vested interest at the expense of the rest of the community, is as a beggar-my-neighbour recipe for prosperity at home, and the Fund maintains that countries should not use exchange control for beggaring their neighbours. Likewise, countries should develop their taxation systems so that they do not have to rely on revenue arising from restrictions in the form, for example, of multiple currency practices.

[1] The quotations are from Article XIV, Section 4 and Article XV, Section 2(*a*).

[2] The I.M.F.'s *First Annual Report on Exchange Restrictions*, p. 22.

[3] *Ibid.*, p. 31.

The Fund's jurisdiction over international restrictions is limited to those affecting international payments. Restrictions on international *trade*, for instance tariffs and import quotas, fall within the province of another Specialized Agency of the United Nations, the International Trade Organization. The document governing the work of the I.T.O. is the so-called Havana Charter,[1] which, besides providing for the creation of the Organization itself, lays down various principles of trade policy to which members must adhere and sets out the procedure to be followed in arranging tariff reductions on a reciprocal basis. The Havana Charter still awaits ratification by a sufficient number of signatories and may very well never come into force, but in the meantime arrangements have been made under the General Agreement on Tariffs and Trade[2] (G.A.T.T.) to pursue the objectives of the Havana Charter. It has therefore rested with the contracting parties of the G.A.T.T. to lead the attack on restrictions falling on trade rather than on payments. Nevertheless the I.M.F. has inevitably been interested in the progress made under the G.A.T.T., since, as we saw in Chapter II, restrictions on payments and on trade are to a large extent similar in their consequences.

> The Fund and the ITO are both primarily concerned with the external economic position of nations—with their balances of payments in the broadest sense. Whereas the Fund approaches the problem of achieving and maintaining a sound external economic position of members primarily from the financial side, the ITO approaches this problem from the viewpoint of commercial policy. The interdependence of these two approaches is obvious and makes full cooperation between the ITO and Fund imperative.
>
> Under its Charter, the ITO will seek agreement with the Fund regarding procedures for consultation on monetary and related questions. A parallel provision is also contained in the General Agreement on Tariffs and Trade.[3]

[1]*Final Act* of the *United Nations Conference on Trade and Employment held at Havana, Cuba, 21st November*, 1947, *to 24th March*, 1948.

[2]See the *Provisional Consolidated Text of the General Agreement on Tariffs and Trade and Texts of Related Documents*, published by H.M.S.O. (Cmd. 8048) in 1950.

[3]*Annual Report,* 1948, pp. 53 and 54.

So far, the G.A.T.T. has achieved more progress than has the I.M.F. Five sessions of the Contracting Parties to the G.A.T.T. have been held, the first at Geneva in 1947, the second at Havana in early 1948, the third at Geneva later in 1948, the fourth at Annecy in 1949 and the fifth at Torquay in 1950. At the first meeting and again at Annecy and Torquay there were long rounds of tariff bargaining, which resulted in very widespread tariff reductions and in numerous undertakings not to raise the existing level of duties.[1]

Moreover, 'in order to protect the value of the [tariff] concessions against measures of indirect protection', such as trade quotas, 'pending the establishment of the I.T.O., many of the commercial safeguards of the draft Charter were incorporated in the Agreement'.[2] The contracting parties are however committed to do no more than apply these safeguards 'to the fullest extent not inconsistent with existing legislation', that is, the various governments are not expected to seek parliamentary approval for undertakings written into the I.T.O. Charter so long as the Charter has not come into force. Subject to this important reservation, it is laid down in the G.A.T.T., as also in the I.T.O. Charter, 'that contracting parties will not resort to the use of quantitative restrictions except for balance-of-payment reasons (and then not without consultation) or after obtaining approval for measures to promote economic development or reconstruction'.

We must however beware of being unduly impressed by the progress apparently achieved under the G.A.T.T. First, many trade quotas and other quantitative restrictions are on a legislative basis, and therefore remain in operation for the time being. Second, many of the items in the impressive list of successful tariff negotiations are merely undertakings to keep

[1]See *The Attack on Trade Barriers*, published by the Interim Commission for the I.T.O., and the *Report on the Torquay Tariff Negotiations*, published in May 1951 by H.M.S.O., Cmd. 8228. The countries represented at Torquay were: Australia, Austria, Belgium, Brazil, Burma, Canada, Ceylon, Chile, Cuba, Czechoslovakia, Denmark, Dominican Republic, Finland, France, Germany, Greece, India, Indonesia, Italy, Luxemburg, the Netherlands, New Zealand, Norway, Pakistan, Peru, the Philippines, Southern Rhodesia, Sweden, Turkey, South Africa, the United Kingdom, the United States, and Uruguay—33 in all.

[2]The quotations in this paragraph are taken from *The Attack on Trade Barriers*, pp. 21 and 26.

within the existing level of duties, not to reduce duties. Third, many of the reductions were in tariffs which were superfluous in that they applied to goods of a kind which would not be imported extensively even without a tariff. Fourth, some of the reductions were in tariffs which were superfluous for another reason, namely that the effective barriers to the import of the dutiable articles were currency restrictions, so that the tariff reductions will have significance only when the currency restrictions are lifted.

So far as currency restrictions are concerned, the Fund Agreement provides that 'Not later than three years after the date on which the Fund begins operations and in each year thereafter, the Fund shall report on the restrictions still in force . . .'[1] under the transitional arrangements. The first of these Reports, which appeared in 1950 and has already been quoted in this chapter, admits on page 26 that:

> In general, progress toward unrestricted current transactions, which the Fund is committed to promote, is not as yet apparent, in spite of some improvements in the underlying conditions which justify hope for more visible progress in the future.

It would seem that the main factors accounting for the lack of progress towards less restricted international payments are as follows:

> First, notwithstanding the Fund's disapproval, payments restrictions have undoubtedly been imposed or retained for reasons unconnected with balance-of-payments problems.
>
> Second, countries imposing payments restrictions for balance-of-payments reasons cannot, without endangering their liquidity, remove their restrictions except in return for reciprocal concessions from other countries, but the Fund (unlike the G.A.T.T.) has not attempted to arrange facilities for achieving an all-round reduction of restrictions by a process of bargaining.
>
> Third, the division of responsibility for the reduction of restrictions as between the Fund and the G.A.T.T. has meant that there have been no suitable facilities to enable countries whose restrictions are mainly on trade to bargain with countries whose most serious restrictions are on payments.

[1]From Article XIV, Section 4.

Fourth, there seems in the post-war world to have been a widespread failure adequately to appreciate the advantages which would accrue from an all-round scaling down of international restrictions. Admittedly it would cause quite disproportionate hardship to seek these advantages by repealing all restrictions overnight, but few countries have shown much enthusiasm even for beginning to tackle the problem in a serious fashion.[1]

### *The Treatment of Disequilibria*

We saw in the previous chapter that the policy of the Fund is to provide additional liquidity, in the form of purchase rights, only for purposes of accommodating temporary disequilibria. Disequilibria which cannot be expected to be self-correcting are not therefore eligible to be accommodated in this way except for limited periods and then only on the understanding that suitable action will be taken to cure or (failing that) to suppress them. We must now consider what in the Fund's view would constitute suitable action.

In general, the Fund's bias is very strongly in favour of curing in preference to merely suppressing disequilibria. All the 'cures' listed at the end of Chapter IV would almost certainly meet with the Fund's approval. First, reduction in the restrictions imposed by surplus countries is required under Article XIV even in the transitional period. Second, the use of exchange controls by deficit countries to prevent 'a large or sustained outflow of capital' is provided for in Article VI, Section 1(*a*); indeed, as we have seen, failure to take such action might render the countries concerned 'ineligible to use the resources of the Fund'. Third, a curtailment of internal demand sufficient to arrest a progressive rise in prices has been constantly advocated by the Fund as an essential part of the cure for external deficits.[2] Finally, the Fund Agreement makes provision, in Article IV, for the change of exchange rates.

Unfortunately however this list of acceptable cures may not be adequate for all circumstances. For first (to take the cures one at a time), though the Fund is empowered to require

[1]This passage is *not* taken from the Fund's *Report*.
[2]See e.g. *Annual Report*, 1949, pp. 4 to 6.

the removal of payments restrictions imposed by surplus countries, it has no direct jurisdiction over trade restrictions. Second, a country's external deficit may not be due to 'an outflow of capital' and even if it were there are serious practical difficulties in the way of preventing such an outflow, as we shall see in Chapter IX. Third, a rising level of prices is doubtless one cause of an external deficit, but it is not the only cause, and a country which has succeeded in preventing its price level from rising may still need to seek other remedies to complete the cure of its deficit. Finally, as we saw in Chapter IV, the restoration of equilibrium by means of adjusting exchange rates is in certain circumstances subject to serious difficulties.

Some of these difficulties have been fully recognized by the Fund. Thus the Fund has stressed that currency depreciation is unlikely to be effective in curing the external deficit of a country suffering from excess demand in the home market, irrespective of whether the result be 'open' inflation, with persistently rising prices,[1] or 'suppressed' inflation, with prices held down by official restrictions.[2] On the other hand the Fund has perhaps not adequately recognized the peculiar difficulties of countries whose economies are inherently inflexible—due, for example, to having highly specialized natural resources. Nor has the Fund paid due attention (at any rate in its public pronouncements) to the danger that the efficacy of exchange rate adjustments may be very seriously reduced when trade and payments are everywhere subject to drastic official restrictions. More adequate recognition should have been given to the fact that in the world as it exists today the cure of disequilibria by means of devaluation (rather than by import restrictions) may require a drastic change of exchange rates and involve the deficit countries in a considerably heavier export burden without any appreciable improvement in export earnings. Devaluation will not become a relatively painless remedy for disequilibria until the Fund and the G.A.T.T. succeed in effecting an all-round removal of restrictions on international payments and trade.

Apart from payments restrictions permitted under the

[1]*Annual Report*, 1948, p. 24.
[2]See M. Gutt's address at Harvard in February 1948.

'transitional provisions' of Article XIV, the only procedure the Fund allows for suppressing, as distinct from curing, international disequilibria is that deriving from the Scarce Currency provisions of Article VII. The first two Sections of this Article deal with the steps to be taken before the final sanction is applied; this sanction is set out in Section 3, as follows:

> (*a*) If it becomes evident to the Fund that the demand for a member's currency seriously threatens the Fund's ability to supply that currency, the Fund, whether or not it has issued a report under Section 1 of this Article, shall formally declare such currency scarce and shall thenceforth apportion its existing and accruing supply of the scarce currency with due regard to the relative needs of members, the general international economic situation, and any other pertinent considerations. The Fund shall also issue a report concerning its action.
>
> (*b*) A formal declaration under (*a*) above shall operate as an authorization to any member, after consultation with the Fund, temporarily to impose limitations on the freedom of exchange operations in the scarce currency.

In addition, under the I.T.O. Charter and the G.A.T.T., one of the exceptions to the proscription of quantitative trade restrictions in general, and discriminatory quantitative trade restrictions in particular, is to permit the use of restrictions having equivalent effect to exchange restrictions authorized under the Scarce Currency Clause.[1]

Thus the formal declaration by the Fund that a member's currency is scarce allows all other members to introduce restrictions on payments and trade directed solely against that member, this discrimination being wisely conceived to prevent the deficit countries from having, quite pointlessly, to impose restrictions against each other.

The main weakness of the Clause is that it cannot be invoked unless a currency seriously threatens to become scarce *in the Fund*, which would not occur, even though the currency were scarce outside the Fund, if for any reason the Fund had decided that the deficit countries were largely ineligible to use its resources. For instance, the U.S. dollar was *de facto* scarce

[1] I.T.O. Charter, Article 23, Section 5(*a*).

outside the Fund for at least three years after the Fund commenced business, but this currency has always been in ample supply within the Fund and has in consequence never become formally scarce.

Admittedly the phrase, 'threatens to become scarce in the Fund' is rather vague in this context, and leaves a margin of discretion to the Fund, and in addition the Fund's discretionary power is increased by the following clause in the I.T.O. Charter:

> No Member shall institute, maintain or intensify import restrictions under this Article except to the extent necessary
> (i) to forestall the imminent threat of, or to stop, a serious decline in its monetary reserves, or
> (ii) in the case of a Member with very low monetary reserves, to achieve a reasonable rate of increase in its reserves[1]

where the interpretation of the key words 'serious', 'very low' and 'reasonable' rests with the Fund.[2] But even so, it is arguable that the Fund is unduly tied by the formula of the Scarce Currency Clause, and should be permitted to declare a formal state of scarcity whenever it decides a currency to be scarce *outside* the Fund.

*The International Transmission of Depressions*

Neither the Fund Agreement nor the Fund's pronouncements since it began business accept that restrictions on payments and trade should ever be imposed for purposes of exporting, or even preventing the import of, business depressions. However, the Fund lays upon its members no obligation to take steps to prevent depression in their respective countries, and therefore offers no assurance that one member may not suffer as the result of another's failure to take such steps.[3] The Australian delegation to the Bretton Woods conference wanted:

[1]From Article 21, Section 3(*a*). The G.A.T.T. incorporates a similar provision.

[2]I.M.F. *Annual Report*, 1948, p. 53.

[3]The only reference in the Fund Agreement to the level of employment is in Article I, where 'the expansion and balanced growth of international trade', is recommended as a means of promoting and maintaining 'high levels of employment and real income'.

> to see Governments specifically accept the obligation to maintain employment. . . . An *agreement* to maintain employment is, of course, only a first step. . . . Nevertheless, acceptance by nations of an obligation to maintain employment would do much to mobilize public opinion to see that the obligation was carried out, and it would give smaller nations, so dependent on the employment levels of others, sufficient confidence to accept obligations that would not otherwise be easy for them.

Perhaps as the result of this protest, the I.T.O. Charter (though not at present the G.A.T.T.[1]) makes concessions to the Australian point of view. These appear in Articles 2, 3 and 6, from which the following are extracts:

> The Members recognize that the avoidance of unemployment or underemployment . . . is not of domestic concern alone, but is also a necessary condition for the achievement of the general purpose and the objectives set forth in Article 1, including the expansion of international trade, and thus for the well-being of all other countries.
>
> The Members recognize that, while the avoidance of unemployment or underemployment must depend primarily on internal measures taken by individual countries, such measures should be supplemented by concerted action under the sponsorship of the Economic and Social Council of the United Nations in collaboration with the appropriate inter-governmental organizations, each of these bodies acting within its respective sphere and consistently with the terms and purposes of its basic instrument.
>
> The Members recognize that the regular exchange of information and views among Members is indispensable for successful co-operation in the field of employment and economic activity and should be facilitated by the Organization.
>
> Measures to sustain employment, production and demand shall be consistent with the other objectives and provisions of this Charter. Members shall seek to avoid measures which would have the effect of creating balance-of-payments difficulties for other countries.
>
> The Organization shall have regard, in the exercise of its functions under other Articles of this Charter, to the need of

[1]The U.S.A. has recently proposed in effect that the I.T.O. should be abandoned but that many of the provisions which appear in the I.T.O. Charter but not the G.A.T.T. should now be included in the latter.

> Members to take action within the provisions of this Charter to safeguard their economies against inflationary or deflationary pressure from abroad. In case of deflationary pressure special consideration shall be given to the consequences for any Member of a serious or abrupt decline in the effective demand of other countries.

These provisions in the I.T.O. Charter include virtually the whole field which was marked out in Chapter V as suitable for international co-operation in anti-depression policies, and even cover the possibility of action to counter the opposite evil of inflation. The main ground for criticism is that the Charter merely states general principles without giving any guide as to how they should be carried out in practice. Nevertheless, it represents a step forward that a whole series of questions which were ignored completely in the Fund Agreement should in the I.T.O. Charter be at least admitted to exist.

Since the time of the Havana conference, at which the I.T.O. Charter was drafted, the only international bodies which have interested themselves in anti-depression measures have been the International Labour Office and the United Nations Economic and Social Council, and the work of these bodies has so far not proceeded much beyond the stage of making rather general recommendations and of exploring suggestions for more definite arrangements.

Perhaps the slowness of progress in this field may be attributed to the quite reasonable belief that the danger of depression is at present much less acute than that of inflation, but unfortunately there is equally little progress to report in the field of international measures for combating inflation. In western Europe, the Organization for European Economic Co-operation has been giving attention to this matter, but has not so far progressed much beyond the stage of studying the problem and making general recommendations. The economists attached to certain United Nations agencies have also undertaken studies of the problem of inflation, but it cannot be said that they have yet aroused much interest among the member countries' governments.

*Conclusion*

The reader will probably share the writer's disappointment at the small amount of progress which has so far been made in realizing the Fund's objectives. Under the heading of 'exchange rates' we had to note the persistence of fairly widespread multiple currency practices. Under 'additional liquidity' we could report that the Fund *qua* banker had done very little business, mainly because it considered most of the post-war disequilibria to be other than 'temporary'. The Fund's unwillingness to do business has inhibited it from furthering its aim of multilateral liquidity, and has rendered the Scarce Currency Clause inoperative, despite the existence of *de facto* scarce currencies. There has been far too little progress towards the Fund's objective of lifting restrictions on current international payments, and its sister organizations have made only slightly more progress in reducing barriers to international trade. In consequence the Fund's best weapon for correcting persistent disequilibria—exchange depreciation—has lost much of its former efficacy and is indeed liable to inflict serious harm on the user. Lastly, the Fund has no authority to concern itself with the international transmission of inflations and depressions.

Many of the Fund's failures have undoubtedly been due to the fact that it has had to bat on a bad wicket: the stresses and strains of the post-war years have been of such unparalleled severity that the new organization has never had the chance of proving its value in relatively normal circumstances.

The major cause of the rather disappointing achievements of the Fund has however been the attitude of its members. Though to the layman the Fund Agreement may seem to be reasonably comprehensive and explicit—indeed even unduly restrictive in certain respects—the text is so imprecise from a legal point of view that a skilful lawyer can make it mean almost anything; hence the value of the Agreement must depend very much on its being respected in the spirit as well as in the letter. In practice there have been grounds for suspicion that in many cases the letter alone has been respected. The Fund's members have tended to regard its charter not as a solemn undertaking which they must constantly strive to fulfil, but rather as something which has to be 'got round' whenever it conflicts with national self-interest. An example of this attitude has been the tenacity that many members have displayed in retaining unnecessary currency restrictions—unnecessary, that is, for the suppression of an external deficit—and the same is true of unnecessary trade restrictions, which (though falling outside the Fund's province) are no less prejudicial to the attainment of the Fund's objectives. This example has been selected because it is so fundamental to the success or failure of the Fund. Drastic and widespread restrictionism is not only itself contrary to the spirit of the Fund Agreement, but also makes the treatment of persistent disequilibria difficult except by resort to further restrictions, and unless persistent disequilibria can be satisfactorily dealt with it is difficult to see how the Fund can begin to operate effectively *qua* banker.

CHAPTER VIII

# EUROPEAN MONETARY CO-OPERATION

FROM the earliest days of the Marshall Plan, both the E.C.A.,[1] the American body administering the Plan, and the O.E.E.C.,[2] the organization set up by the beneficiaries, have taken the line that the cautious policy of the I.M.F. made it desirable to supplement the Fund with western European machinery designed both to provide additional liquidity to accommodate specifically intra-European disequilibria and also to facilitate the correction of these disequilibria.

After the liberation of Europe, the revival of intra-European trade had been almost solely on the basis of bilateral payments agreements under which one of the partners, or each of them, undertook to grant limited accumulation facilities to the other. The simplest way of describing these agreements is to say that in effect one country, say Belgium, allowed her partner, say Britain, limited rights to settle in her own currency, sterling; but the actual wording of the agreements described the arrangement in a more roundabout way, the Belgian monetary authorities undertaking to 'sell Belgian francs to the Bank of England . . . against sterling'[3] so that British deficits with Belgium could (to the extent permitted by the agreed 'swing') be settled in Belgium's currency.

A survey of these bilateral payments agreements is given in the eighteenth *Annual Report* of the Bank for International Settlements (published in 1948), which tells us that they

> were usually concluded between governments, according to a fairly uniform pattern: the central banks, as technical agents, supplied their own currency at a fixed rate of exchange against that of their partner up to a certain limit, which was often referred

[1]Economic Co-operation Administration.
[2]Organization for European Economic Co-operation.
[3]From the Anglo-Belgian *Monetary Agreement* of November 1947, published by H.M.S.O., Cmd. 7264.

> to as the 'swing', since it was intended to afford room for minor fluctuations in commercial deliveries between the two countries; beyond the limit thus fixed settlements had generally to be made in gold or convertible currency.[1]

By October 1947, however, it was reported[2] that

> the margins of credit possible under the payments agreements concluded by some countries are almost exhausted, and this is a quasi-permanent situation. For the expansion of trade to the extent which is possible, increasingly numerous gold payments would be necessary. This situation risks hampering not only the development of trade, but actually its maintenance at the present level. . . . In these circumstances, the Committee considers that greater flexibility in the present payments system is more than ever necessary.

This need for greater flexibility was the motive behind the Agreement on Multilateral Monetary Compensation of November 1947, which came into being largely as the result of the work of the Committee of European Economic Co-operation, the committee which also brought the O.E.E.C. into being in April 1948. Fourteen of the O.E.E.C. members were parties to the Agreement, but only six (Belgium, Luxemburg, France, Italy, Netherlands and the Bizone of Germany) were 'permanent' members; the other eight were 'occasional' members, with the right to contract out of any operation arising under the Agreement.[3] The operations provided for in the Agreement were 'first-category compensations' and 'second-category compensations'. From the description of these processes which is given us by the official Agent of the Agreement, the Bank for International Settlements,[4] we see that the former comprise circular offsetting, while the latter comprise non-circular settlements between two countries achieved by transferring a third country's currency:

[1]'Convertible currency' here means currency which the issuing country is always prepared to exchange against gold.

[2]By the Committee on Payments Agreements, which was set up by the recipients of Marshall Aid. Quoted in the 18th *Annual Report* of the B.I.S., p. 146.

[3]The occasional members were: Austria, Denmark, Greece, Norway, Portugal, Sweden, the United Kingdom and the French Zone of Germany.

[4]See the 18th *Annual Report* of the B.I.S., pp. 148–9.

> First-category compensations involve only a reduction of existing balances ("balances" in this context covering both debit and credit accounts). Such operations imply a "closed circuit" of countries each of which is debtor to its immediately preceding partner, while it is itself a creditor of its succeeding partner, the last country in the chain being the creditor of the first country, thus closing the circuit. These operations are partially automatic (in so far as the "permanent" countries are concerned) and partially optional (in so far as they apply to "occasional" members). . . . The simple offsetting . . . of the first category can lead only to reductions of outstanding debts (and credits) and presents no particular difficulties—except that, in some cases, countries may for one reason or another desire to maintain certain balances in one or more particular markets and thus are unwilling to reduce them. . . .
>
> A "second-category operation" may be defined as a payment made by one country to another by utilising the currency of a third country. A simple example would be the payment of a Norwegian debt to the Netherlands in sterling. It is evident that such a transaction involves a limited transferability of sterling.

Unfortunately, the category of operations which was easier to effect was possible in only a comparatively small number of cases.

> The working accounts of the European payments agreements show debts (and credits) entering into the compensations to the equivalent of over 700 million dollars. About 400 million of this total is net debt (or credit) which cannot be offset.[1] Of the 300 million which can be subject to compensation in theory, experience has shown that, at the present time, the maximum possibilities of the first category alone amount to about 30–50 million. From this it follows that the possibilities for the reduction of debts (and credits) by operations of the second category are some ten times as great as those of the first category.

As a result only a very limited amount of first category compensation was possible. Second category compensation was in practice also very restricted, for it was optional even in the case of 'permanent' members and almost all the proposals were objected to by the country whose currency was to be

[1]'Net debt (or credit)' corresponds, in the language of Chapter III, to 'overall deficit (or surplus)'.

transferred, for reasons which were explained in Chapter III. In the event only $5 millions of first category compensations and $46 millions of second category compensations had been effected when the scheme was superseded in October 1948 by the first Intra-European Payments Scheme.[1]

*The Intra-European Payments Schemes*

The first I.E.P.S., which operated for the nine months October 1948–June 1949, differed from the preceding arrangement in that it involved all the O.E.E.C. countries and also incorporated provisions for Indirect Aid. The provisions for first and second category compensations were retained, the former being compulsory,[2] the latter remaining optional, but during the nine months that the scheme was in operation very few compensations were in fact effected.

Indirect Aid was so called because the E.C.A. made a portion of the Marshall Aid extended to certain O.E.E.C. countries conditional on their undertaking to extend similar aid to other O.E.E.C. countries. The motive of the E.C.A. in recommending, and indeed in insisting on, the Indirect Aid provisions of the I.E.P.S. was to increase the amount of aid going to the most needy European countries, for each $1 of aid granted was supposed to benefit both the immediate recipient and the indirect recipient, each to the extent of $1.[3] But though the primary purpose of Indirect Aid was to assist the reconstruction of the European countries whose economies had been most upset by the war, the help was provided in a form which made a direct contribution to the external liquidity of the recipient countries. The countries through whom Indirect Aid was granted were those which were expected to run surpluses with other O.E.E.C. countries during the period of the Scheme, and the aid they granted took the form of bilateral drawing rights in favour of each of the

[1]*Agreement for Intra-European Payments and Compensations*, 1948, published by H.M.S.O., Cmd. 7546.

[2]Except for Switzerland and Portugal.

[3]Indirect Aid was the second device used by the E.C.A. to facilitate intra-European aid, for during part of 1948 the E.C.A. made 'off-shore' purchases for dollars in various European countries and delivered them as Aid to other countries. This technique was however soon abandoned.

countries with whom a bilateral surplus was expected.[1] Each deficit country should, in theory, have received the necessary means of settlement for covering each of its nine-monthly bilateral deficits with the other O.E.E.C. countries. In practice, as we shall see, this objective was far from being fully achieved, for the forecasts of bilateral relationships were necessarily rather wild guesses, and the rigid bilateralism of the drawing rights prevented them from being utilized where they were actually needed, as distinct from where they were expected to be needed. Even where the estimates did prove reasonably accurate, this may merely have meant that countries simply adjusted their import regulations from time to time so as to make their bilateral deficits run according to plan.[2] Countries certainly had an incentive to act in this way, for the I.E.P.S. offered them no inducement to eliminate their deficits.

The total of the drawing rights provided for was initially the equivalent of 810 million U.S. dollars (later revised to $805 millions), but in the event only $677 millions were used before the termination of the Scheme, and of this amount $67 millions were used for purposes other than meeting deficits. In addition to granting a portion of these drawing rights, Britain made a further contribution by agreeing that certain other O.E.E.C. countries should draw on their sterling balances to a predetermined extent.[3]

The Indirect Aid drawing rights were in effect vicarious gifts from the United States, for the countries receiving the rights gave no *quid pro quo*, while the countries affording the rights were reimbursed by Conditional Aid from the E.C.A. It is interesting to note that in practice Conditional Aid turned out to be unconditional, in that the countries affording drawing rights which were not wholly utilized suffered no reduction in their Conditional Aid and the unused drawing rights were

[1]Neither Switzerland nor Portugal participated in Indirect Aid under the first I.E.P.S., but only Switzerland did not participate under the second I.E.P.S.

[2]See G. D. A. MacDougall's article in the London and Cambridge Economic Service *Bulletin* of August 1950.

[3]Similar contributions were offered by several other countries, but much smaller in amount than Britain's.

either cancelled or carried forward to the 1949–50 scheme.

The second Intra-European Payments Scheme, for the year July 1949 to June 1950, followed its predecessor closely except that the total of drawing rights was somewhat increased and rather over one quarter of them was multilateral, i.e. capable of being used to settle bilateral deficits with any of the participating countries. (In most of the drawing rights granted, 25 per cent, or thereabouts, was multilateral, but the rights granted by Belgium were more than half multilateral.) The 'multilateralizing' of over one quarter of the drawing rights was a distinct advance over the 1948–49 scheme, but given the other provisions of the Schemes, it introduced new dangers. Under both the schemes the countries granting vicarious aid were to be reimbursed with Conditional Marshall Aid, and though in 1948–49 the Conditional Aid turned out in the event to be unconditional, it was understood that in 1949–50 the conditional character of such Aid was to be insisted upon, and in particular that a country A, granting multilateral drawing rights to B, would get its corresponding Conditional Aid only if B actually drew on A; if B drew on C instead, C would to that extent get A's Conditional Aid. Hence, under the 1949–50 scheme it was most important for a country granting drawing rights to achieve a surplus at least equal to, and preferably greater than, the amount of the drawing rights, even if this meant imposing additional restrictions on imports. Thus there was the danger that this scheme, whose main purpose was to facilitate intra-European trade, might in fact do the opposite. As it turned out, the restrictive effect of the scheme was not serious, presumably because only a proportion of the drawing rights was multilateral,[1] and because the multilateral portions of the drawing rights were to be used only after the B.I.S. had performed all possible first category compensations and had then made the fullest use of bilateral drawing rights.

The tables which follow, Tables 6 and 7, summarize some of the more important information collected by the B.I.S. in the course of operating the two Payments Schemes over the

[1]It had at first been suggested that a much higher percentage of the rights should be multilateral, but due to the fear of restricting trade the proportion was whittled down in the course of the negotiations. See *Economist*, 2nd July, 1949, p. 31.

whole 21 months from October 1948 to June 1950. Columns 1 and 2 of the former table set out the B.I.S.'s figures of the total of the *bilateral* deficits and surpluses of each participating country[1] with each of the other participants *in each separate month.* The bilateral deficit or surplus of any one participant with any other participant in each month was calculated by the B.I.S. by simply noting the monthly movements of each country's official holding of the other's currency, before the B.I.S. had arranged any end-of-the-month adjustments in the form of Indirect Aid, of first and second category compensations, and of gold or dollar settlements. Thus the United Kingdom's bilateral deficit with Belgium in (say) January 1949 would comprise the month's change in Belgium's official holding of sterling, minus the month's change in the United Kingdom's official holding of Belgian francs. The bilateral deficits and surpluses on which Table 6 is based thus conform to the definitions adopted in Chapter III, except in cases when movements in one participant's holding of another's currency were due to receipts from, or payments to, a third country. Such cases would occur in practice mainly as a result of the widespread use of sterling for making settlements outside the United Kingdom. If, for example, Belgium settled with Brazil in sterling this would not concern the United Kingdom's 'true' bilateral deficit with Belgium, as defined in Chapter III, but it would reduce the U.K.-Belgian deficit as calculated by the B.I.S.[2] (The fact that the B.I.S. calculates

[1]Switzerland is however excluded, since she did not take part in Indirect Aid.

Eire and Iceland, being members of the Sterling Area, are not shown separately from the U.K. Likewise Luxemburg is included with Belgium and Trieste with Italy.

[2]If Belgium's settlement in sterling had been not with Brazil but with another participant, say France, but the settlement was not made through the machinery of the I.E.P.S. (so that the B.I.S. did not record the transaction as a second-category compensation) the B.I.S.'s figures of each of the bilateral deficits between the three countries concerned (Belgium, France and Britain) would differ from the 'true' deficits.

According to the Bank of England's *Report* for the year ended 28th February, 1950, p. 10, £48 millions of sterling were in 1949 transferred by O.E.E.C. countries to other countries outside the Sterling Area, £100 millions were received by O.E.E.C. countries from outside the Sterling Area, and £48 millions were transferred between Britain's fellow members of the O.E.E.C.

## TABLE 6

INTRA-EUROPEAN PAYMENTS SCHEMES

DEFICITS AND SURPLUSES AS BETWEEN THE PARTICIPATING COUNTRIES, OCTOBER 1948–JUNE 1950
(*All figures are expressed to the nearest million*[1] *of U.S. dollars*)

| Country | Total of *Monthly* Bilateral Deficits and Surpluses with each of the other Participants | | 'Reciprocal' Deficits and Surpluses | Total of Bilateral Deficits and Surpluses, *taking the Period as a whole* | | Overall Deficit or Surplus with all other Participants, *taking the Period as a whole* | |
|---|---|---|---|---|---|---|---|
| | Deficits | Surpluses | | Deficits | Surpluses | Deficit | Surplus |
| | 1 | 2 | 3 | 4 | 5 | 6 | 7 |
| Austria .. .. | 170 | 12 | 7 | 163 | 5 | 158 | |
| Belgium .. | 151 | 722 | 151 | — | 570 | | 570 |
| Denmark.. .. | 201 | 174 | 122 | 79 | 51 | 28 | |
| France .. .. | 453 | 454 | 296 | 157 | 158 | | 1 |
| Greece .. .. | 241 | 7 | 7 | 233 | — | 233 | |
| Italy .. .. | 107 | 412 | 96 | 11 | 316 | | 305 |
| Netherlands .. | 552 | 298 | 186 | 366 | 112 | 254 | |
| Norway .. .. | 260 | 41 | 32 | 228 | 10 | 218 | |
| Portugal .. | 139 | 47 | 30 | 109 | 16 | 93 | |
| Sweden .. .. | 143 | 300 | 103 | 40 | 197 | | 157 |
| Turkey .. .. | 161 | 83 | 63 | 98 | 20 | 78 | |
| United Kingdom | 946 | 1,025 | 544 | 402 | 481 | | 79 |
| Western Germany | 502 | 452 | 260 | 242 | 192 | 50 | |
| Total .. | 4,025 | 4,025 | 1,897 | 2,128 | 2,128 | 1,112 | 1,112 |

[1]In this and later tables the process of rounding leads to small discrepancies in the additions.

## TABLE 7

### INTRA-EUROPEAN PAYMENTS SCHEMES
### DRAWING RIGHTS UTILIZED TO MEET DEFICITS,
### OCTOBER 1948 TO JUNE 1950

(*All figures expressed to the nearest million of U.S. dollars*)

| Country | On a Bilateral Basis | | On an Overall Basis | |
|---|---|---|---|---|
| | Amount Received | Amount Granted | Amount Received | Amount Granted |
| | 1 | 2 | 3 | 4 |
| Austria .. | 152 | 4 | 148 | |
| Belgium .. .. | 9 | 434[1] | | 425 |
| Denmark .. | 35 | 7 | 28 | |
| France .. .. | 321 | 56 | 265 | |
| Greece .. .. | 199 | 0 | 199 | |
| Italy .. .. | 0 | 80 | | 80 |
| Netherlands .. | 206 | 32 | 175 | |
| Norway .. .. | 131 | 11 | 120 | |
| Portugal .. | 16 | 3 | 13 | |
| Sweden .. .. | 8 | 85 | | 77 |
| Turkey .. .. | 75 | 34 | 41 | |
| United Kingdom | 62 | 362 | | 300 |
| Western Germany | 106 | 213 | | 107 |
| Total .. | 1,319 | 1,319 | 989 | 989 |

bilateral deficits and surpluses in this way has important consequences in the working of the European Payments Union, as we shall see later on in this chapter.)

The figures in Columns 4 and 5 of Table 6, relating to the bilateral deficits and surpluses of each participant with each of the other participants *taking the 21-month period as a whole* are less than the totals of *monthly* bilateral deficits and surpluses (Columns 1 and 2) since the process of cumulation gives rise to a considerable amount of cancellation. For

[1]Including drawings on the loans which Belgium made available, in addition to Drawing Rights proper, under the second I.E.P.S.

example, in some of the 21 separate months the United Kingdom had bilateral deficits with Belgium (total $148 millions) while in the other months of the period Belgium had bilateral deficits with the United Kingdom (total $44 millions); in Column 1 *all* these deficits would appear—$148 millions as part of the United Kingdom total and $44 millions as part of the Belgian total—but in Column 4 only the United Kingdom deficit for the period as a whole ($104 millions) would be recorded. In general terms, the difference between the two columns arises from what may be termed 'reciprocal deficits'—i.e. from bilateral deficits of A with B in some months balanced by bilateral deficits of B with A in other months. The total of 'reciprocal deficits' is shown in Column 3, and since a reciprocal deficit is (by definition) one which is balanced by a surplus in the same bilateral relationship, the same column also serves to show the total of reciprocal surpluses (accounting for the difference between Columns 2 and 5).

Columns 6 and 7 of Table 6 have been calculated as the differences between Columns 4 and 5, and thus give the *overall* deficit or surplus of each participant with all the other participants in the 21-month period as a whole. If we refer to the last line of Column 6, we see that the total overall deficits among the participants in the 21-month period as a whole was $1,112 millions, whereas the total of bilateral deficits was on the same basis $2,128 millions, so that the total of 'compensable' deficits was some $1,000 millions. However, only very little of this last amount—less than $100 millions in fact—was covered by first and second category compensations arranged under the I.E.P.S.; this must be attributed partly to the fact that deficits only rarely occurred in closed circuits, partly to the reluctance of countries to allow their currencies to be transferred.[1]

The second of the two tables, Table 7, summarizes the Indirect Aid operations under the two Schemes. The point

[1]It will be recalled from footnote 2 on p. 102 that in addition to the second-category compensations arranged under the I.E.P.S. there were other transfers of sterling of a second-category type—i.e. as between two of Britain's fellow members of the I.E.P.S. Such transfers effected outside the I.E.P.S. machinery were not included in the B.I.S.'s statistics of first and second category compensations.

which calls for comment is the apparent inadequacy of the amount of drawing rights actually utilized to cover deficits, namely $1,319 millions on a bilateral basis, or $989 millions on an overall basis. Admittedly the latter amount was not far short of the total of overall deficits ($1,112 millions), but since so little was achieved under the I.E.P.S. provisions for first and second category compensations a large amount of bilateral drawing rights could usefully have been provided in addition to complete the clearing of the compensable deficits. This indeed seems to have been the intention of the Payments Schemes, but it was only very imperfectly realized, as will be seen by comparing the total of $1,319 millions of bilateral rights utilized with the total of $2,128 millions of bilateral deficits shown in Column 4 of Table 6. Even this comparison is however too favourable, for about $250 millions of the $1,319 millions of bilateral rights utilized were used to cover reciprocal deficits.[1]

In view of the apparent inadequacy of the drawing rights available under the two schemes, it was unfortunate that some of the rights originally provided for had to be cancelled or left unused. The first scheme was particularly liable to be 'wasteful' of drawing rights, since these were established on a rigid bilateral basis, which meant that rights which in the event proved to be over-generous could not be used elsewhere. Rather surprisingly, a somewhat larger amount was 'wasted' under the second scheme, even though a portion of the drawing rights was multilateral; an explanation is perhaps to be found in the changes in exchange rates which occurred in September 1949,[2] which considerably altered the previous pattern of intra-European deficits.

[1]It was not intended in principle that any reciprocal deficits should be covered by Indirect Aid but:

(i) if we consider the two Payments Schemes together (as we have been doing) we find a few cases of drawing rights arranged, and used, reciprocally. The amount used served to cover about $40 millions of reciprocal deficits;

(ii) in other cases, totalling about $210 millions, drawing rights were used to meet bilateral deficits which were later balanced by bilateral surpluses, without however any repayment of the drawings. (This explains e.g. why France's bilateral drawings in Column 1 of Table 7 exceed her bilateral deficits in Column 4 of Table 6.)

[2]See below, Chapter XI.

*The European Payments Union—Liquidity Provisions*

The next scheme for intra-European payments, the European Payments Union (E.P.U.),[1] though carrying on some features of its predecessors, is much more nearly comparable, in its aims and its machinery, with the I.M.F. than with the previous European schemes. First, the 'aid' provisions of the 1948–49 and 1949–50 schemes reappear under the alias of 'Initial Credit (and Debit) Positions', but their total amount is only about $300 million.[2] Second, the little used provisions in the I.E.P.S. for first and second category compensations are rendered unnecessary by a system of pooled and fully multilateral drawing rights, which *automatically* clear all compensable deficits, irrespective of their size. Third, the drawing rights which a deficit country enjoys under the E.P.U. (unlike those available under the I.E.P.S.) are *automatically* replenished when in any month the country achieves a surplus; thus the means for settling 'reciprocal deficits' is provided *as required* under the E.P.U. instead of inadequately (and indeed unintentionally) under the I.E.P.S. Fourth, the E.P.U. agreement, again unlike the I.E.P.S., includes provisions designed to correct, as well as to accommodate, intra-European disequilibria.

Basically the arrangement for pooling drawing rights is that each member has been allotted a '*quota*',[3] and undertakes to extend to the Union an overdraft right equal to 20 per cent of his quota. In return the Union extends a reciprocal overdraft right to the member, again equal to 20 per cent of the member's quota, and this reciprocal right is exercisable in the currency of any other Union member. The Union can offer the reciprocal right to the member by virtue of the rights which the Union enjoys against all the other members.

The Union's unit of account in its transactions is the same as the I.M.F.'s, namely the equivalent of 0.888671 grams of fine gold, which corresponds to the present par value of the U.S. dollar. The Union pays interest on the overdraft facilities

[1]The Agreement has been published by H.M.S.O. See *Documents Relating to the E.P.U.* and *Agreement for the Establishment of an E.P.U.*, Cmd. 8064.

[2]This is the approximate total of the credit positions; the total of the debit positions is less—namely $215 millions.

[3]See Table 8 on p. 108.

### TABLE 8

LIST OF MEMBERS OF THE E.P.U., WITH THEIR RESPECTIVE QUOTAS
(*expressed in millions of U.S. dollars*)

| Country | Quotas |
|---|---|
| Austria | 70 |
| Belgium | 360 |
| Denmark | 195 |
| France | 520 |
| Germany | 320 |
| Greece | 45 |
| Iceland | 15 |
| Italy | 205 |
| Netherlands | 330 |
| Norway | 200 |
| Portugal | 70 |
| Sweden | 260 |
| Switzerland | 250 |
| Turkey | 50 |
| U.K. | 1,060 |
| TOTAL | 3,950 |

it has used, at a rate of 2 per cent per annum, and charges on the overdrafts which it accords to members 2 to 2½ per cent on the amount taken, depending on the period the amount has been outstanding.

It will be seen that the main difference in the *modus operandi* of the E.P.U. and the I.M.F. is that in the former the members do not pay subscriptions to, but offer overdraft facilities to, the central authority, and in return they enjoy not purchase rights (as in the I.M.F.) but overdraft rights. These however are differences only of machinery, not of substance. The chief differences of substance are that under the E.P.U. the drawing rights are virtually unconditional for both current and capital payments, and that the E.P.U.'s techniques for limiting the use of its facilities are more flexible than the Fund's.

Under the E.P.U. the limitation of drawing rights is achieved in effect by allowing a member to overdraw from the Union more than 20 per cent of his quota, provided that his drawings in excess of this amount are supplemented by his purchasing from the Union, for gold or U.S. dollars,[1] a certain proportion of his foreign currency[2] requirement. The proportion of a member's foreign currency requirement that he must pay for in gold or dollars depends on a formula which will be described below. The proportion thus prescribed is only a minimum: any member is free to exceed it.

The gold or dollars which the Union obtains from the members who obtain foreign currencies from it will be roughly balanced by disbursements to the members from whom the Union obtains these currencies. For the Union in its turn can draw on a member in excess of 20 per cent of his quota, provided that the Union supplements such drawings by purchasing from him, for gold or dollars,[3] an appropriate proportion of the Union's requirement of his currency. To provide for the contingency that the Union's receipts of gold and dollars may fall short of its payments, the E.C.A. has provided it with a 'kitty' of 350 million U.S. dollars.

It is likely that in practice the Union will be dealing with most (or even all) of its members on a two-way basis: that is, the typical member will sometimes engage in deals which make him a debtor to the Union (when he obtains foreign currency from the Union) and at other times in deals which make him a creditor (when he supplies his own currency to the Union). It has however been arranged that the B.I.S., as the Union's agent, shall record each member's 'cumulative net position', i.e. his overall deficit or surplus with all the other members as from mid-1950,[4] and that in all transactions of the Union, whether the Union is obtaining from a member an amount of his currency or supplying to him an amount of foreign currency,

[1]The Union can accept another currency in lieu at its discretion.

[2]The foreign currencies which a member may obtain from the Union are of course confined to the currencies of the other members of the Union.

[3]The Union can alternatively pay in some other currency acceptable to the creditor-member.

[4]These deficits and surpluses are to be calculated on exactly the same basis as those shown above in Table 6.

the proportion of the amount which has to be paid for in gold and dollars shall depend solely on the member's cumulative net position and on a single scale of proportions, reproduced below as Table 9.

## TABLE 9

SCALE FOR DETERMINING, FOR ANY TRANSACTION OF THE E.P.U., THE PROPORTION WHICH REQUIRES SETTLEMENT IN GOLD OR DOLLARS

DEFICIT MEMBERS

| Cumulative Net Position of the Member Concerned, dating from mid-1950 | Proportion of *additional* Currency received or supplied by the Union needing to be paid for in gold or U.S. dollars |
|---|---|
| | *Per Cent* |
| Deficit in excess of member's quota . . | 100 |
| Deficit between 80 and 100% of member's quota . . . . . . | 80 |
| Deficit between 60 and 80% of member's quota . . . . . . | 60 |
| Deficit between 40 and 60% of member's quota . . . . . . | 40 |
| Deficit between 20 and 40% of member's quota . . . . . . | 20 |
| Deficit between 0 and 20% of member's quota . . . . . . | 0 |

SURPLUS MEMBERS

| Cumulative Net Position of the Member Concerned, dating from mid-1950 | Proportion of *additional* Currency received or supplied by the Union needing to be paid for in gold or U.S. dollars |
|---|---|
| | *Per Cent* |
| Surplus between 0 and 20% of member's quota . . . . . . | 0 |
| Surplus between 20 and 100% of member's quota . . . . . . | 50 |
| Surplus in excess of member's quota | not specified |

It will be seen that the *modus operandi* of the Union is such that the facilities made available to members are not subject to a fixed maximum amount, as in the case of the I.M.F.; instead the Union member with an increasing deficit position is subject to gradually increasing pressure to correct his deficit.

The significance of the principle on which the E.P.U. formula for gold payments is based will be seen if we contrast it with the principle on which gold payments had previously been required under the bilateral agreements, with two-way swings, which linked many of the members of the I.E.P.S. Under her bilateral agreement with (say) Belgium, Britain would lose gold if her cumulative bilateral deficit with Belgium took her to the limit of the agreed swing, and this gold would never come back to Britain unless she thereafter ran a surplus large enough and persistent enough not only to wipe out her cumulative deficit but also to build up a cumulative surplus in excess of the swing. Thus gold lost under a bilateral agreement did not normally begin to return for a long time, if at all. On the other hand, gold losses to the E.P.U. begin to return immediately a member has a current surplus in any single month, i.e. he begins to get gold back without having to eliminate his cumulative deficit, let alone build up a cumulative surplus.

It is now appropriate to mention several subsidiary provisions in the E.P.U. agreement, relating to settlements between one member and another.

First, any two members of the Union who have a bilateral payments agreement can continue to make settlements outside the Union, but the gold payments by and to the Union are the same whether credit is granted and received bilaterally or through the Union.[1] Moreover the provisions for the liquidation of the Union (should this occur) are such that the 'share out' will be precisely the same whether previous settlements have been through bilateral agreements or through the Union. In practice no members have so far chosen to settle outside the Union, and it is difficult to see why any should want to in the future.

Second, the equivalent of Indirect Aid under the E.P.U. is to be arranged by giving the vicarious providers of the Aid 'Initial

[1]See Cmd. 8064, Article XII.

Debit Positions' in the Union and the recipients 'Initial Credit Positions'; thus such Aid will be part of the ordinary settlement machinery and will therefore be fully multilateral.

Third, if a member has an amount of his currency or of his liquid debts held by other members as at 30th June, 1950, due e.g. to the operation of earlier monetary agreements, he must be prepared either to make an agreement to amortize the balances or to allow them to be used by the holders as 'existing resources' for settling any net deficit with the Union. Any balance which is given the status of 'existing resources' therefore corresponds broadly to an initial net creditor position for the holder and to an initial net debtor position for the other party. The main balances to be settled under these provisions are the sterling balances of various members, particularly Italy, Sweden and Portugal, the total amount of which on the date in question was about £200 millions. Britain has indicated that she is prepared that all this sterling may be used for settling deficits with the E.P.U. and much of it has already been so used. If (as has indeed actually happened) the use of sterling 'existing resources' should involve Britain in gold payments to the Union, she is (by a special agreement) to be reimbursed by the E.C.A.

A practical example of how settlements are effected under the E.P.U. is given in Table 10, which summarizes the first nine months' operations. Column 1 of the table shows the cumulative overall surplus (marked +) or deficit (marked —) of each member country with all the other members, taken together. As in Table 6, the total of the overall surpluses is necessarily equal to the total of the overall deficits. Column 2 shows the amount of existing resources which deficit countries holding such resources chose to use in settling with the E.P.U. (marked —) and the amount and 'nationality' of the currencies which the E.P.U. thereby acquired (marked +). The excess of Column 1 over Column 2 was used, as shown in Column 3, to cancel an equivalent amount of a deficit country's initial credit position (marked —) or of a surplus country's initial debit position (marked +), to the extent that such initial positions had been created. In so far, however, as initial positions (*a*) had not been created, or (*b*) had been created in the wrong sense—i.e. if a deficit country had been provided with an initial debit position, or vice versa, or (c) were inadequate to meet the excess of Column 1 over Column 2, a balance remained (Column 4) corresponding to the amount of the member's quota utilized, whether by the member against the Union (marked —) or by the Union against the member (marked +). This balance had to be settled by the exercise of drawing rights (Column 6) or in gold or dollars (Column 7). In this way the whole of each country's overall surplus or deficit was settled.

## TABLE 10

E.P.U. OPERATIONS, JULY 1950–MARCH 1951

(*All figures are expressed to the nearest million U.S. dollars*)

| Overall Surplus (+) or Deficit (—) | Use of Existing Resources | Use of Initial Position | Column 1 *minus* Columns 2 and 3 | Country | Amount of Quota Utilized | | |
|---|---|---|---|---|---|---|---|
| | | | | | Credit | Gold | Total |
| 1 | 2 | 3 | 4 | 5 | 6 | 7 | 8 |
| — 83 | | — 80 | — 3 | Austria .. .. | | — 3 | — 3 |
| + 90 | —16 | + 44 | + 61 | Belgium .. | + 61 | | + 61 |
| — 41 | — 2 | | — 39 | Denmark .. | — 39 | | — 39 |
| +271 | + 1 | | +270 | France .. .. | +187 | + 83 | +270 |
| —457 | —12 | | —446 | Germany .. | —272[1] | —174 | —446 |
| — 94 | — 1 | — 93 | 0 | Greece .. .. | | | |
| — 4 | | — 4 | 0 | Iceland .. .. | | | |
| — 84 | —43 | | — 41 | Italy .. .. | — 41 | | — 41 |
| —193 | | — 30 | —163 | Netherlands .. | —119 | — 44 | —163 |
| — 74 | | — 60 | — 14 | Norway .. | — 14 | | — 14 |
| + 63 | | | + 63 | Portugal .. | + 39 | + 25 | + 63 |
| — 46 | —15 | | — 30 | Sweden .. | — 30 | | — 30 |
| + 27 | | | + 27 | Switzerland[2] .. | + 27 | | + 27 |
| — 11 | + 2 | | — 13 | Turkey .. .. | — 12 | — 1 | — 13 |
| +634 | +86 | +150 | +398 | U.K. .. .. | +305 | + 93 | +398 |
| ±1,085 | ±89 | +194<br>—267 | +821<br>—748 | TOTAL .. | +619<br>—527 | +202<br>—221 | +821<br>—748 |

[1]This figure includes $80 millions drawn against a 'Special Credit' of $120 millions extended to Germany after she had reached the limit of her quota.

[2]November 1950—March 1951 only.

It should be noted that Table 10 merely shows how the E.P.U. countries settled their overall deficits or surpluses over the 9-month period as a whole. In addition to the total of $1,085 millions of overall deficits (or surpluses) shown in Table 10 there was in the 9 months a further total of $1,260 millions of 'reciprocal' deficits and 'compensable' deficits. Both reciprocal and compensable deficits are however cleared *automatically* under the E.P.U., for the following reasons:

1. Since E.P.U. drawing rights are available to meet a deficit country's *cumulative* net position, a deficit country's outstanding drawing rights are automatically replenished when in any month the country achieves a surplus. Moreover, as we have already seen, if the deficit country has had to pay gold to the Union, the gold begins to flow back whenever the monthly deficits give place to monthly surpluses. In other words, the repaying of 'temporary accommodation' completely restores the *status quo*.
2. If we neglect settlements made in gold or with 'existing resources',[1] what a member of the Union is required to do is to cancel at the end of each month all the bilateral debts which are due from him and to him, in return for an equivalent change in the Union's debt to him or in his debt to the Union; and whether a member's bilateral deficit (or surplus) was with Belgium or with Turkey makes not the least difference once it has been transformed into a debt to (or from) the Union.

But why, it may be asked, were the countries which joined the Union prepared to see their bilateral debts and credits thus transformed? Take first the case of a country which expected to run an overall surplus with the other members. Such a country has under the E.P.U. to exchange claims to sterling and other European currencies for a claim on the Union

[1]Settlements in gold or in 'existing resources' are however arranged under the E.P.U. in a way which does not upset the multilateral basis of settlements through the Union. Gold transactions arise when a member reaches a certain critical 'cumulative net position' (in one direction or the other) *with the Union*; his position in relation to any particular other member is of no consequence. 'Existing resources' can be used to settle *any* debt to the Union; thus Italy could use sterling 'existing resources' to clear her debts to the Union even though she was not running a bilateral deficit with Britain.

expressed in dollars. This claim on the Union is however only *expressed* in dollars; it is not necessarily a claim to dollars. What a claim on the Union does amount to can only be understood from a careful reading of the very complicated provisions governing the rights and obligations of members in case of their withdrawal from the Union or in case of the complete liquidation of the Union.[1]

Very briefly these provisions are aimed at (a) making it relatively unprofitable for a member to withdraw individually; (b) giving the creditor members of the Union, if it were ever decided to liquidate the Union, first a claim to the Union's gold and dollars, including what remains of the 'kitty' supplied by the E.C.A., and second a right to have the greater part of the balance of their credit paid to them by the larger and more stable member countries; and (c) giving the debtor members, on liquidation, the right to discharge their debts to the Union in the currencies of the other Union members,[2] not in dollars, and to spread a considerable part of the repayments over a period of not less than fifteen years. It may seem remarkable that the liquidation provisions of the Union should have been drafted so as to satisfy both the countries which expected to be overall creditors and the countries which expected to be overall debtors, but the task of reconciling the two sides was of course greatly facilitated by the gift of $350 millions from the E.C.A.

Anyway, whatever may be the reasons which prevailed upon the O.E.E.C. countries to agree to pool their bilateral debts, the fact that they have agreed to pool them, through the machinery of the E.P.U., means that these countries now comprise an area in which full multilateral settlement is not only possible but automatic. It does not, for instance, make the least difference to the British monetary authorities whether British tourists choose to visit Switzerland rather than Norway, whether British importers buy in Germany or in Greece, or whether British exports go to Holland or to Belgium—though

[1]Annex B of Cmd. 8064, and Annex III of *Documents Relating to the E.P.U.*

[2]The proportion to be repaid in each currency depends on complicated formulae, the outcome of which is difficult to predict.

prior to the E.P.U. there was a strong incentive for preferring the latter alternative in each of the three examples, as being much the less likely to cause an outflow of gold.

Moreover, owing to the way in which the B.I.S. calculates surpluses and deficits,[1] the effective area of multilateral settlement is—subject to certain reservations which are mentioned below—very much greater than that comprised by the European members of the O.E.E.C., owing to the fact that several members' currencies are the usual, or even the sole, media for making international settlements in other large areas of the world. Of the western European currencies thus used for making international settlements, sterling is much the most important, as we shall see in Chapter IX, and it is therefore appropriate to illustrate our argument with reference to this currency.[2]

Let us take France as typifying any O.E.E.C. country outside the Sterling Area, Australia any country of the outer Sterling Area and Brazil any country outside both the Sterling and O.E.E.C. areas which is nevertheless prepared to accept settlements in sterling. Then the extent to which Australia and Brazil are effectively within the O.E.E.C. multilateral settlement area can be investigated by considering the question from the point of view of each of the countries concerned.

> *France* has no monetary incentive to prefer making payments to (or getting receipts from) Australia rather than Britain, since her sterling holdings (and therefore her cumulative net position with the E.P.U.) will be affected in precisely the same way in the two cases. This statement remains true if we substitute Brazil for Australia, provided that France settles with Brazil in sterling and not in francs under a Franco-Brazilian bilateral agreement.
>
> *Britain* has an incentive to prefer a bilateral deficit with Australia to one with France, unless she expects Australia to spend her sterling earnings in the O.E.E.C. area or in some other country which is unwilling to accumulate much more sterling.[3]

[1]See above, p. 102.

[2]It should be noted however that the Belgian, Dutch, French and Portuguese currencies are used extensively, or even exclusively, as means of settlement within their respective colonial empires.

[3]This assumes that Australia does not become so surfeited with sterling as to be liable to leave the Sterling Area altogether.

This statement remains true moreover if Brazil is substituted for Australia, provided that Britain is not in danger (under her bilateral agreement with Brazil) of reaching the limit of the permitted swing. Britain has an incentive to prefer a bilateral surplus with France rather than with Australia, and with France rather than with Brazil unless Brazil has run short of sterling and has therefore to settle in dollars.[1]

*Australia* will in any case settle in sterling, but a bilateral deficit with France would favour an outflow of gold from the Sterling Area pool to the E.P.U., which would not be true of a bilateral deficit with Britain or (unless the Anglo-Brazilian agreement were near the end of its swing) of a bilateral deficit with Brazil.

*Brazil* would normally settle with Britain and Australia in sterling. She could also settle in sterling with France, unless (which is very unlikely) the British exchange control refused to authorise the transfer of sterling, but she might prefer to pay France in francs if she had accumulated francs under a bilateral agreement.

The status with respect to the E.P.U. of Australia and Brazil is thus rather complicated, and the same is true of all non-European countries using Western European currencies as media for settlements. We can however say *first* that in many cases an E.P.U. member will deal with Australia or Brazil exactly as with a fellow member of the E.P.U., and *second* that in circumstances where a member does have ground for discrimination his bias will almost always be towards increasing his deficit (or reducing his surplus) with Australia or Brazil rather than with another E.P.U. member. This rule is of course in marked contrast with the incentives which the E.P.U. gives to its members (so long as the dollar is a hard currency) to give priority to reductions in their deficits (or increases in their surpluses) with the United States and with other countries which accept settlements only in gold and dollars. This incentive to sell in America and spend in Europe, whenever there is a dollar shortage, is of course entirely commendable; all that can be said against the E.P.U. arrange-

[1]The Anglo-Brazilian agreement does not require Britain to accept Brazilian currency.

ments in this connection is that the incentive operates erratically, since the proportion of any monthly settlement with the Union which needs to be made in gold or dollars has been made to vary considerably with the net cumulative position of the member concerned (see Table 9). As a result the pressure to sell in America rather than Europe and to buy in Europe rather than America will at any time be considerably different for different E.P.U. members and also for the same member in different months.[1]

### *The E.P.U.—Correction of Disequilibria*

The E.P.U. is however not simply a scheme for providing additional liquidity to accommodate intra-European disequilibria; it is also, unlike the I.E.P.S., an agreement to correct such disequilibria. The relevant provisions[2] can be summarized thus:

> First, as we have seen, the provisions requiring considerable debtors to settle in gold or dollars provides them with an incentive, lacking entirely under the I.E.P.S., to correct their external deficits.
>
> Second, restrictions on trade are to be reduced. A separate O.E.E.C. scheme, involving all the E.P.U. members, requires each country to 'liberalize' (i.e. to free from all quantitative restrictions) 60 per cent of its imports on private account from other member countries.[3] This liberalization is advan-

[1]See R. F. Kahn's article on the E.P.U. in *Economica*, August 1950.

[2]See Sections IV and V of *Documents relating to the E.P.U.*

[3]The decision to liberalize trade between the O.E.E.C. countries in this way dates back to a proposal made by Sir Stafford Cripps at an O.E.E.C. meeting in June 1949. (*Economist*, 2nd July, 1949, p. 32.) This proposal crystallized into an O.E.E.C. decision that countries should 'liberalize' 50 per cent of their trade by 15th December, 1949, or show good reasons why this was impossible.

The 50 per cent target applied separately to 'food and feeding stuffs, raw materials, and manufactured goods'. According to the O.E.E.C.'s *Second Report* of February 1950 (p. 224), 'most member countries have reached, or even exceeded, the targets thus laid down'. A further resolution was adopted by the O.E.E.C. in January 1950, to the effect that 'member countries must make it their aim to remove, as soon as . . . a Payments Scheme comes into force, quantitative restrictions on at least 60 per cent of their imports on private account from other member countries taken as a group'. (*Second Report*, p. 226.)

tageous,[1] not only because it facilities international specialization on the basis of comparative costs, but also because it increases the value of the I.M.F. provisions for exchange rate adjustments to correct international disequilibria.

Third, the E.P.U., by putting liquidity on a fully multilateral basis, makes it unnecessary for members to discriminate in respect of their imports as between one member and another. Hence members undertake to avoid such discrimination.

Fourth, an exception to the rule of non-discrimination is provided in the form of the equivalent of the I.M.F.'s Scarce Currency Clause, allowing for discrimination against a member who has achieved a creditor position in excess of 100 per cent of his quota. The value of this provision is of course greatly enhanced by the fact that drawing rights against the E.P.U. (unlike those against the I.M.F.) are unconditional, so that if a member's currency becomes *de facto* scarce it will also become formally scarce.

Fifth, there is in the E.P.U. Agreement a contrary provision to deal with the deficit country whose debtor position comes to exceed 100 per cent of its quota. A country in this situation 'may suspend on a temporary basis measures taken by it for the liberalization of trade'.[2]

Taken together, the E.P.U. Agreement itself and the associated scheme for the liberalization of trade represent an ambitious attempt to do for western Europe what the I.M.F. and G.A.T.T. have left undone. This has involved the provision of additional liquidity, on a multilateral basis and with a workable equivalent to the I.M.F.'s Scarce Currency Clause, while at the same time providing an incentive to deficit countries to adopt corrective measures. It has also involved an attack on quantitative restrictions on trade, a field in which the G.A.T.T. has progressed less rapidly than in the reduction of tariffs.

[1]It is however only a small beginning, since (1) only *private* trade is affected and (2) a country with 60 per cent of its imports 'liberalized' may nevertheless be continuing to pursue a highly restrictive policy, since the non-liberalized 40 per cent of its imports may comprise a very extensive range of goods on which its post-war restrictions have been so drastic that only a small quantity of each was in fact imported in the base year (1948).

[2]This clause actually became operative for Germany in 1951, and for the U.K. and France early in 1952.

## CHAPTER IX

# STERLING[1]

STERLING deserves an important place in a study of international monetary co-operation, first because even in the post-war period (and *a fortiori* before the war) it had a much stronger claim than any other currency to be called an *international* currency, second because the British monetary authorities have consciously used it as a means of international monetary co-operation,[2] and third because the techniques of the Sterling Area exchange controls provide an illuminating case study of what can (and what cannot) be done by restrictions of this kind.

A study of the international role of sterling is however rendered difficult by the absence of any 'written constitution' comparable with the 'charters' of the I.M.F., the E.P.U., and the predecessors of the E.P.U. Moreover the sterling machinery has actually worked to a much greater extent than has the I.M.F. machinery, or the machinery of the various European payments schemes. For these reasons the present chapter will involve more history and less 'constitutional theory' than the previous three chapters, and will thus provide a suitable introduction to the actual course of events since the end of the war.

### *Sterling under the Gold Standard*

The gold standard was neither invented nor consciously planned. It grew up gradually as a gold currency standard in the eighteenth and nineteenth centuries, gaining more and more adherents with the passage of time and enjoying its

[1]I am indebted to the editor for permission to reproduce in this chapter extracts from my article on 'Sterling as an International Currency', which appeared in the June 1948 issue of the *Economic Record*.

[2]In Sir Stafford Cripps's words, 'We are intent on maintaining the largest possible area of multilateral trading on the basis of sterling'. (Board of Trade Journal, 1st January, 1949, p. 4.)

heyday from the end of the Franco-Prussian War (when the German Empire adopted gold as its standard) until the outbreak of the First World War. The standard suffered a partial eclipse as the result of that war, but was revived in the nineteen-twenties as a gold bullion standard, only to collapse, more or less completely, in the early nineteen-thirties.

Both versions of the gold standard have already been described in Chapter II, but only in their bare essentials, so that certain important practical features were passed over without comment. One such practical feature was the role of sterling in the working of the standard. Any realistic description of the mechanism of international payments under either version of the gold standard must recognize that in practice gold accepted sterling as in some respects an equal, or even superior, partner. Certainly sterling was much the more *active* partner, for unlike gold it could be transferred from one country to another almost without expense. But sterling was also prized almost equally with gold as an asset suitable for holding as a store of value, and in the case of many countries, not only the working balances of the commercial banks, but also part or even the whole of the official reserve of the central bank, were kept in the form of sterling.

Why, under the gold standard, was sterling so widely used as an international currency? *First*, Britain had a voracious appetite for imports and (partly in consequence of this) British investors were willing to make considerable overseas loans, with the object of developing the export potential of Britain's suppliers. As a result, the whole world was constantly supplied with sterling: there was no tendency for Britain to develop a persistent overall surplus. *Second*, since Britain's overseas loans were sterling loans, the borrowing countries committed themselves to meet a debt service in sterling, and this naturally provided a strong inducement to hold a reserve of sterling. *Third*, since many countries had an extensive import trade with Britain, it was quite convenient for them to conduct at least a considerable proportion of their overseas transactions in sterling, and to hold working balances in London. *Fourth*, the sterling prices of British goods were reasonably stable, so that there was no great danger that working balances or official reserves of sterling would suffer a severe depreciation in purchasing power. *Fifth*, sterling was almost continuously convertible into gold by virtue of the Bank of England's willingness to buy and sell gold freely at a fixed price. *Sixth*, sterling could be lent in London with complete safety and thus earn interest. *Seventh*, sterling enjoyed unrestricted transferability, and this, in conjunction with London's unrivalled credit facilities, the acceptance houses and bill market, made the bill on London, a sterling bill, the world-wide instrument for financing international trade. Prior to the First World War the three months bill on London was used almost in the role of an international bank-note. *Eighth*, the currencies of such countries as would *not* accept sterling without limit could always be bought as required in London. Thus there was no need for (say) Australia to hold stocks of marks or francs, or even to hold stocks of gold with which to buy these currencies; she could always get them whenever she needed by buying them for sterling. These eight reasons are surely adequate to explain the widespread use of sterling as an international currency under the gold standard.

### *The Pre-war Sterling Area*

Early in the nineteen-thirties the gold standard virtually collapsed; most countries apart from the Gold Bloc (France, Italy, Switzerland, Holland and Belgium) gave up the attempt to maintain a stable exchange rate with gold. The seceding countries were, however, for the most part keenly aware of the disadvantages of freely fluctuating exchange rates, and many of them chose to stabilize the value of their currencies in relation either to sterling or to the U.S. dollar, both of which were then completely unrestricted in their transferability. (Indeed before the war, exchange control in any form was very rare outside Germany, Italy, the U.S.S.R. and the eastern European countries.[1]) The countries which decided in favour of a stable exchange rate with sterling came to be known as the Sterling Area, which by 1933 comprised the whole of the British Empire except Canada and Newfoundland, most

[1]Certain other countries temporarily imposed controls on capital payments in the early 1930s.

of the Scandinavian and Baltic countries and a few others.[1]

To the countries which joined the Sterling Area the transition from the gold standard to the new regime involved little change in their monetary policy. They still declared an official exchange rate, though now not with gold but with sterling. Their official reserves now consisted almost entirely of sterling, not gold,[2] but for most members of the area this did not involve any considerable departure from their practice under the gold standard. Their official agencies also bought and sold sterling freely at the official rate, just as previously they had bought and sold gold.[3] The *modus operandi* of the Sterling Area was indeed so similar to that of the gold standard that we may reasonably describe the members of the area as adhering to the sterling *standard.*[4] Perhaps the only important departure from the rules of the gold standard was that the members of the Sterling Area did not commit themselves to continue indefinitely with their original official rates of exchange. However, though each member country reserved its right to prevent an undue depletion or accumulation of its sterling reserves by the device (taboo under the gold standard) of simply varying its official exchange rate, in practice the members of the area rarely if ever availed themselves of this right.

We see then that after the collapse of the gold standard a considerable part of the world retained sterling in use as an international currency. What of the rest of the world? The banks of countries outside the Sterling Area continued their practice, which had grown up under the gold standard, of keeping most, or even all, of their working balances in the form of sterling. Moreover, sterling was in use throughout the world as much the most popular means of making inter-

[1]The Sterling Area eventually included the Colonial Empire and Mandates, the Southern Dominions, Eire, Egypt, India, Iraq, Portugal, Siam, Iran, Estonia, Sweden, Norway, Finland, Denmark and Latvia.

[2]South Africa, though regarded as a member of the Sterling Area, continued to keep her official reserves mainly in the form of gold. She held sterling only as a working balance.

[3]Even under the gold standard, certain of the countries which later joined the Sterling Area had made effective their official exchange rates with gold by buying and selling sterling (which could be exchanged for gold in London) freely at the appropriate price. Such countries were said to be on the gold *exchange* standard.

[4]See above, p. 47.

national payments, as it had been under the gold standard. For indeed the attractiveness of sterling as an asset and as a means of payment had been little diminished by Britain's departure from the gold standard. Though in the years 1931–34 sterling had depreciated by some 40 per cent in relation to the gold bloc currencies which had not been devalued (e.g. the French and Belgian francs), it had maintained its value in relation to other currencies, and the subsequent devaluations of the gold bloc currencies reduced the relative depreciation of sterling to only about 20 per cent.[1] Moreover sterling was not in this period subject to short period fluctuations in value, thanks to the operations of the Exchange Equalization Account, whose *modus operandi* was briefly described in Chapter II.[2] Finally sterling remained throughout a fully acceptable means of settlement with the extensive Sterling Area. It is not therefore surprising that right up to the time that war became imminent, sterling should remain in world-wide use as a means of international settlement.

### *War Time*

In the early stages of the war the Sterling Area lost all its European members and soon came to consist only of the British Empire (excluding Canada and Newfoundland), Egypt and the Sudan, Iraq, Iceland and the Faroes. When the exigencies of war demanded the official rationing of international payments the Sterling Area countries concentrated mainly on controlling payments into and out of the Sterling

[1]According to the footnote on p. 129 of *International Currency Experience*, published by the League of Nations in 1944, the value in sterling of other currencies changed as follows after Britain left the gold standard in 1931. All figures are percentages of the exchange rates prevailing in December 1930.

| Country's currency | 1932 | 1934 | 1936 |
|---|---|---|---|
| Argentine | 113 | 97 | 97 |
| Brazil | 120 | 84 | 90 |
| Australia | 73 | 86 | 86 |
| Sweden | 100 | 93 | 93 |
| India | 100 | 100 | 100 |
| Canada | 130 | 99 | 99 |
| U.S.A. | 149 | 98 | 99 |
| Czechoslovakia | 149 | 139 | 118 |
| Italy | 149 | 159 | 99 |
| Belgium | 149 | 165 | 120 |
| France | 149 | 165 | 118 |

[2]Page 26.

Area *as a whole*, leaving payments between one Sterling Area country and another almost entirely free.[1] There was however no single authority responsible for exchange control in the Sterling Area, for the Dominions within the Area retained full autonomy and only the U.K. and the Colonial controls were responsible to Whitehall. The autonomy of the Dominion members of the Area was such that they retained three rights: they could freely authorize the transfer of sterling to any part of the Sterling Area, they could also authorize the transfer of sterling to non-sterling countries, and they enjoyed unrestricted access to the Exchange Equalization Account in London for converting their sterling into gold or into U.S. dollars. Naturally the second and third of these rights were used with due restraint. The Exchange Equalization Account itself underwent a certain change of function: instead of continuing as the official agency for buying and selling sterling in the gold and foreign currency markets it became, once these markets were made illegal, simply the Sterling Area's common pool of gold and foreign currencies (more particularly U.S. dollars).

The U.K. exchange control operated by canalizing all exchange transactions through 'authorized dealers', namely the Bank of England, the Joint Stock banks, and a number of merchant banks and acceptance houses, all of which were permitted to deal with all countries, and the London offices of various Dominion, Colonial and foreign banks, each of which was permitted to deal with one overseas country or a limited number of countries. Apart from the Exchange Equalization Account, these dealers became the only authorized holders of foreign currencies; any foreign currency acquired by any other British resident had immediately to be sold to them for sterling.[2]

[1]The U.K. control did not restrict payments within the Sterling Area at all. Some Dominions had such restrictions, but they were very mild in practice.

[2]The only relaxation which has been made in this provision was made in December 1950, in respect of the Scandinavian countries. Exporters to these countries may now retain their earnings of the three currencies concerned.

It may also be noted that Sterling Area residents were permitted to accept payment from non-residents only in sterling and in certain so-called 'specified' currencies. The specified currencies in January 1952 are as indicated in Table 11, on p. 136.

Moreover the authorized dealers, and they alone, could (a) buy and sell foreign currencies for sterling, (b) get gold and foreign currencies (in particular dollars) from the Exchange Equalization Account,[1] (c) transfer sterling as between the account of a U.K. resident and that of a resident in a foreign country, and (d) transfer sterling as between the account of a resident in one foreign country and that of a resident in another foreign country. The word 'foreign', in this connection, means 'outside the Sterling Area', for the transfer of sterling within the Area, was not subject to the British control. In addition the authorized dealers became legally the sole intermediaries in the export and import of bank-notes and of negotiable securities. By virtue of these measures, the authorized dealers, and they alone, were in a position to exchange sterling against gold and foreign currencies;[2] they also controlled all inward and outward sterling payments between residents of the United Kingdom (but not of the outer Sterling Area) and foreigners, and the transferability of sterling as between different foreign countries. This machinery for exchange control, set up early in the war, has remained substantially unchanged to the present day.

How was the machinery used? First, in its dealings with the other Sterling Area exchange controls, the British dealers simply transferred sterling on request. Second, all transactions between United Kingdom residents and foreigners were subject to the closest scrutiny and vetoed if the war effort so demanded. Third, transfers of sterling as between residents of different foreign countries were in many cases restricted. Fourth, foreigners were made to accept payments from the Sterling

[1]Prior to 1951 the Account had nearly equal buying and selling prices for each 'specified' currency when doing business with the authorized dealers. In December, 1951, however (and somewhat earlier in the case of the Canadian dollar), the Account slightly widened the margin between its buying and selling rates and permitted the authorized dealers to deal in foreign currencies among themselves. For example, in the case of U.S. dollars the Account had previously sold dollars at 2.79⅞ per £ and bought them at 2.80⅛ per £, and this spread was widened to 2.78—2.82 (approximately the maximum spread allowed by the I.M.F.): in consequence U.S. dollars henceforth changed hands between authorized dealers, and between them and the public, at a price which fluctuated within the limits of 2.78—2.82 per £. The change of policy did not however imply any relaxation of the British exchange control regulations, as they affected the public (whether here or abroad).

[2]Except for the black markets. See below, pp. 141–148.

Area exclusively in sterling and only in certain cases did they enjoy a right of conversion—i.e. of getting gold or dollars for their sterling, at the official selling price, from the Exchange Equalization Account.[1]

In practice the British control, like the other Sterling Area controls, came to distinguish between foreign countries which would accept inconvertible sterling and those which would not. This was the historical origin of the distinction between 'soft' and 'hard' currency countries.[2] In dealing with a hard currency country (like the United States or Canada) the Sterling Area controls would be less likely to authorize a transaction involving a payment by the Area, and more likely to authorize one involving a receipt by the Area, than in dealing with a soft currency country. Moreover, though the sterling held by hard currency countries was transferable almost without restriction and freely convertible into U.S. dollars, the sterling accounts of other countries were mostly subject to a system of currency control known as the *Special Accounts* system. The sterling earnings of the countries in question were paid into Special Accounts, and sterling in Special Accounts was not convertible into gold or dollars and could not normally be used for making international payments except to the Sterling Area. There were some exceptions to the latter restriction: for instance country X might be allowed to draw freely on its Special Account to make payments not only to the Sterling Area but also to certain specified countries Y and Z[3] and even to make payments to other countries if the transaction requiring the payment had been specifically approved by the British exchange control. But apart from these relatively minor relaxations, the Special Accounts system virtually put an end to the use of sterling for making payments between two soft currency countries outside the Sterling Area,

[1]Only foreign banks classified as authorized dealers had direct access to the Exchange Equalization Account, but other holders of convertible sterling could have access through an authorized dealer.

[2]See above, p. 43.

[3]Thus the Special Accounts arranged for the Central American countries, the so-called Central American Accounts, permitted each Central American country to spend its sterling earnings either in the Sterling Area or in any other Central American country. The Central American Accounts were however unusual in the number of choices open to the holders.

and thus considerably detracted from the usefulness of holding sterling.

Why during the war period were many allied and neutral countries willing to accept sterling with all the limitations imposed by the Special Account system? They did so to a certain extent because they wanted to use it to buy imports, but in many cases this was not the whole explanation, for certain countries (e.g., Argentina) had such a large export surplus with the Sterling Area that their willingness to accept sterling in practice implied a willingness to accumulate sterling. Some of these countries in fact accumulated very large sterling balances in the course of the war. Their willingness to do this partly reflected their faith in the value of sterling after the war, but it must also be remembered that at this time Britain was the only large market for these countries' exports.

*Post-war Changes*

After the liberation of Europe the British Government took a very active part in the negotiation of the bilateral agreements, to which reference was made at the beginning of the previous chapter. In particular, agreements were concluded with Belgium, Czechoslovakia, Denmark, France, Holland, Norway, Portugal, Sweden and Switzerland. These agreements, though by no means identical in their terms, followed a fairly uniform pattern: they all provided for a fixed rate of exchange, and in each case Britain's partner undertook to accept sterling from the Sterling Area and in return was permitted to use its sterling freely to make payments to the Sterling Area. The post-liberation agreements thus to some extent followed the model of the war-time Special Accounts, but not however in all respects. In the first place most of the new agreements incorporated a so-called 'gold clause', which prescribed maximum 'swings' beyond which each party's requirement of the other's currency had to be settled in gold. The 'swings' permitted by the agreements were frequently different in the two directions, Britain undertaking to accumulate her partner's currency up to the equivalent of X dollars, and her partner to accumulate sterling to the equivalent of Y dollars. The other important difference between the post-war agreements and the war-time

Special Accounts was that the former were less strictly bilateral than the latter, since provision was frequently made for fostering transferability on an administrative basis, as opportunity offered.

The next steps which were taken to reinstate sterling as an international currency were the result of the Anglo-American Loan Agreement, which was negotiated in 1945 and came into force on 15th July, 1946. Under Sections 7, 8(i) and 8(ii) of this Agreement,[1] Britain committed herself to abolish her exchange restrictions on current transactions much sooner than the end of the Transitional Arrangements under the I.M.F. Agreement.[2] Section 8(i), which became operative immediately, precluded the United Kingdom from imposing restrictions on payments and transfers, for current transactions, from the United Kingdom to the United States, or on the use of virtually all sterling owned by U.S. residents. (Section 8(i) did not however preclude Britain from imposing quantitative trade restrictions, as distinct from exchange restrictions, on imports from the U.S.A.,[3] though Section 9 required that after the end of 1946 such restrictions should be applied, with certain exceptions, in a non-discriminatory manner.) Section 8(ii), which was to become operative one year after the Agreement came into force, precluded the United Kingdom from imposing 'restrictions on payments and transfers for current transactions' from the United Kingdom to any other country, with the following exceptions:

> First, restrictions were permitted if imposed in conformity with the I.M.F. Agreement (e.g. under the Scarce Currency Clause, or by special authorization of the Fund under Article VIII).
>
> Second, the United States government could waive the United Kingdom's undertaking in exceptional cases.
>
> Third, restrictions were permitted if needed 'to uncover and dispose of assets of Germany and Japan.'
>
> Fourth, restrictions were permitted on the use of sterling already held by third countries and their nationals.

[1]Published by H.M.S.O. as a White Paper in 1945.

[2]See above, Chapter VII.

[3]See article by Knapp and Tamagna, *Sterling in Multilateral Trade*, in the Federal Reserve Bulletin, September 1947.

The fate of the sterling balances already in existence was dealt with in Section 10 of the Agreement, which provided that such balances should either be 'adjusted as a contribution to the settlement of war and post-war indebtedness and in recognition of the benefits which the countries concerned might be expected to gain from such a settlement', or 'be released at once and convertible into any currency for current transactions' or blocked initially but released in a similar manner over a period of years.

The last section we have to consider, Section 7, which was also to become operative one year after the Agreement came into force, was addressed to Britain as custodian of the whole Sterling Area's gold and foreign currency reserve, and required that (with one minor exception) 'the sterling receipts from current transactions of all sterling area countries . . . will be freely available for current transactions in any currency area without discrimination'.

Britain worked to implement the provisions of the Loan Agreement mainly by means of two devices, *American Accounts* and *Transferable Accounts*. The former accounts were arranged, mostly in 1945, with the United States, the Philippines, Colombia, Costa Rica, Cuba, Bolivia, the Dominican Republic, Ecuador, El Salvador, Guatemala, Haïti, Honduras, Mexico, Nicaragua, Panama, Venezuela, Chile and Peru. (The last two named countries subsequently left the American Account area.) The Transferable Accounts were negotiated mainly in the first half of 1947, with the following countries: Argentina, Brazil, Uruguay, Belgium, Holland, Portugal, Spain, Norway, Finland, Italy, Czechoslovakia, Egypt and the Sudan, Iran, Ethiopia, Sweden, Canada and Newfoundland. Thus the countries of the world could in July 1947 be grouped roughly under four headings: The Sterling Area, the American Account Area, the Transferable Account Area, and 'all others'.

So far as the Sterling Area was concerned the implementation of the Loan Agreement required that the United Kingdom and Colonial exchange controls should lift any restrictions which had hitherto been imposed on current payments to countries outside the Area, and that the United Kingdom should eliminate all discrimination against the United States in her quantitative trade restrictions. At the same time the Dominion members of the Area were of course free to follow suit if they chose to do so.

With regard to the American Account Area, the Loan Agreement was implemented by permitting current payments to be made into American Accounts both from accounts of residents of the Sterling Area and from Transferable Accounts, and by providing that the British authorities should on demand freely convert into U.S. dollars all sterling paid into American Accounts.

Transferable Account arrangements worked in a more complicated fashion than those for American Accounts, for unlike American Accounts they incorporated provisions aimed at fostering the use of sterling as an international currency. Let us consider the Transferable Account arrangements which would have been made with an imaginary country, Ruritania. First of all, if Ruritania was a country which had, during the war, accumulated a large balance of sterling, there would probably be an arrangement to block part of this balance, or to hypothecate it for some specified purpose. Then there would be an undertaking by Ruritania to accept sterling from all other countries in settlement of current (though not capital) transactions. In return Britain would offer Ruritania important concessions. Ruritania would be permitted to draw freely on the sterling 'at the disposal' of her monetary authorities (i.e. on the sterling accruing to the new Ruritania Transferable Accounts from future current transactions or from existing balances which had not been blocked) to make *current* payments to virtually all countries,[1] including the American Account countries. This last concession, the right to transfer sterling for current purposes to American Accounts, was of course of great significance, since the British authorities were committed to convert into dollars all the sterling thus transferred.

Thus the Transferable Account countries, unlike the Dollar Area countries, in effect agreed to use *and hold* sterling as an international currency. First, they agreed to accept sterling

[1]The countries to whom current payments could not be made freely were the miscellaneous group referred to on p. 132 with the exception of the countries listed in footnote 3 on that page.

from all countries in payment for exports or for any other current purposes. Second, they agreed to retain the sterling they earned until such time as they needed to use it for buying imports or making other current payments.[1] In effect therefore they committed themselves to sterling both as a means of international payment and as an international store of value.

The miscellaneous group of countries which we have labelled 'all others' had not by July 1947 been brought within the provisions of the Loan Agreement. This group included one country (Switzerland) which preferred to continue on the basis of her bilateral agreement, certain bilateral agreement countries with whom (it was hoped) Transferable Accounts would soon be negotiated,[2] two ex-enemy countries (Germany and Japan) whose overseas payments were still controlled in detail by the Allies, and finally a small residual group of countries which were unable or unwilling to operate an effective exchange control.[3]

The provisions in Section 10 of the Loan Agreement, concerning the treatment of already existing sterling balances of overseas countries, were not closely adhered to. At the middle of 1947 about £3½ billions were outstanding[4] (mostly in the form of British Treasury Bills), of which about one half was covered by short-term blocking arrangements. None of the balances had been cancelled (and indeed none have since been cancelled, apart from the £46 million gifts from Australia and New Zealand). Nor had any of the blocking arrangements been put on a long term basis (though here there has recently been a certain amount of progress). Hence there was in July 1947 a vast amount of 'old' sterling in existence which either had the full status of 'current' sterling or had this status withheld merely by short-term agreements.

[1]However, a number of countries had Transferable Accounts agreements which provided for a limited 'swing', beyond which settlement had to be made in some means other than sterling (usually gold or U.S. dollars).

[2]The United States granted a postponement until 15th September, 1947, of Britain's obligations under the Loan Agreement in respect of fourteen countries: Austria, Bulgaria, China, Denmark, France, Greece, Hungary, Paraguay, Poland, Roumania, Thailand, Turkey, the U.S.S.R., Yugoslavia.

[3]The principal countries in this group were Afghanistan, Albania, Korea, Liberia, Nepal, Saudi Arabia, Cyrenaica, Eritrea, Tripolitania and Yemen.

[4]The comparable pre-war figure was £½ billion.

The measures which were taken for increasing the transferability of sterling were followed by such a drain on the Sterling Area gold and dollar reserve that on 20th August, 1947, after consulting the United States government, Britain suspended the right of Transferable Account countries to use sterling from their Transferable Accounts for making current payments to American Accounts. How did this suspension of convertibility affect the three major areas: the Transferable Account Area itself, the Sterling Area and the American Account Area? To take the last Area first, the legal rights attaching to American Accounts were unaffected, for all sterling accruing to these accounts could still be freely converted into dollars. But it was no longer possible for the American Account countries to earn sterling from the Transferable Account countries. The *Sterling Area* was not directly affected by the suspension of convertibility, but the world-wide dollar shortage, of which the suspension of convertibility was a symptom, was a most serious matter to most Sterling Area countries and led to certain changes in the Area's currency arrangements. In particular, South Africa decided to modify the war-time procedure under which her exports of gold were always sold in London for sterling,[1] and Sterling Area countries generally agreed to limit their dollar expenditure in accordance with principles arrived at in discussion with the British government. (In certain cases, for example Eire and India, expenditure was for a time limited by agreement to fixed annual amounts.)

A later development, affecting both the American Account Area and the Sterling Area, was the reimposition by the latter of discriminatory restrictions directed against the United States. The Dominion members of the Sterling Area were of course free agents in this matter but Britain was tied by the

[1]South Africa has a large output of new gold, almost all of which is retained in her official reserves or exported. During the period that she was selling her gold exports exclusively to Britain, she made payments to other countries exclusively by drawing on her sterling holdings. Under an agreement negotiated in October 1947 South Africa undertook to sell in London only such gold as was required to meet her sterling deficit and to make a loan of £80 millions; the rest of her gold exports could at her discretion be sold elsewhere, for example in the United States. (There have since been modifications in the agreement which provide for increased sales of South African gold in London.)

Loan Agreement. Britain however claimed that discrimination in favour of her colonies was not a breach of the Agreement[1] and in fact reintroduced such discrimination towards the end of 1947. More recently the United States has supported the schemes (to which reference was made in Chapter VIII) for liberalizing trade in western Europe, and have agreed that Britain (and her colonies) should participate in them, even though they require her to discriminate in favour of imports from her fellow members of the O.E.E.C.

With regard to the *Transferable Account* countries, the suspension of convertibility was so serious a matter that the relevant payments arrangements had in effect to be renegotiated. Some of the countries went back to their earlier 'bilateral' status, modified in most cases by 'administrative transferability'. This meant that such countries would accept sterling, at any rate up to a prearranged swing, in settlement from the Sterling Area and could in turn always use their sterling to make payments to the Sterling Area, but that other transfers of sterling to them or from them were subject to the approval of both their own monetary authorities and the British exchange control. The other countries in question continued with their Transferable Account arrangements, with however the important difference that their sterling could now be transferred automatically only to the Sterling Area and to other Transferable Account countries: transfers to other countries were henceforth at best only on an administrative basis and in the case of American Account countries were prohibited altogether.

The countries which continued their Transferable Account status after the suspension of convertibility in August 1947, and those which acquired this status later on, were broadly speaking those whose monetary authorities could be trusted to keep to the new and more stringent rules of the Transferable Account game, and whose sterling receipts and payments could be expected to stay reasonably in balance. The British monetary authorities were not inclined to give Transferable

[1]The British case is based on the doctrine that members of a group of countries which have, like Britain and her colonies, a common quota in the I.M.F. should be entitled to discriminate in favour of one another against countries outside the group when the group as a whole is in balance-of-payments difficulties.

Account status to countries which would have tended to be persistently short of sterling (e.g. Greece[1]), since the difficulty which such countries already had in settling their accounts with the Sterling Area would have been aggravated if they had been free to settle in sterling outside this Area. Nor, on the other hand, did the British authorities want to give Transferable Account status to countries which would have tended to accumulate sterling persistently. This was particularly the case where a country required settlement in gold beyond a limited swing (as in the case of Belgium, Portugal or Switzerland, for example[2]), but even in other cases a Transferable Account arrangement would have caused difficulties both to Britain and to the country concerned. Take for example Argentina. Argentina tended in the period after August 1947 to accumulate sterling almost to the point of satiety, so that she had no desire to incur an obligation to accept sterling from countries outside the Sterling Areas, and Britain for her part was also anxious to restrict transfers of sterling to Argentina, for the more Argentina was satiated with sterling the less ready she would be to continue her supplies of meat and other products to the British market. (Of course transfers of sterling *from* Argentina did not give rise to comparable difficulties and were in fact frequently permitted on an administrative basis.)

The developments which occurred immediately after 20th August, 1947, resulted in the regrouping of the countries of the world under four headings,[3] from the point of view of the transferability of sterling. The membership of each group has changed from time to time and is now as set out in Table 11. The characteristics of each group can be summarized briefly as follows, so far as unblocked sterling is concerned:

*The Sterling Area.* Within this Area unconditional transferability is the rule, qualified by certain local controls mainly on capital transactions. Payments into the Area are unrestricted and can always be made in sterling. Payments out of the Area

[1]Greece has however recently been given Transferable Account status.

[2]A more extreme example was Canada, where (as in the period before 1947) the monetary authorities would not undertake to accumulate sterling, so that the Sterling Area had to settle with Canada in gold or in Canadian or U.S. dollars.

[3]Plus most of the 'small residual group' listed in footnote 3, p. 132.

require authorization by the British or the local controls, according to the domicile of the payer. In the case of the United Kingdom, the exchange control on capital transactions and on imports of services (e.g. tourists' expenditure) is strict, but permission to pay for imports of goods is automatic if an import licence has been obtained.[1] Thus the effective restrictions are largely restrictions on trade rather than on payments and the same is true of most of the other countries of the Area.

*American Account Countries.* Once sterling has reached an

## TABLE 11

STATUS OF COUNTRIES IN JANUARY 1952 WITH REGARD TO THE TRANSFERABILITY OF STERLING

| *Sterling Area* | *American Account Countries* |
|---|---|
| The United Kingdom | *United States and her Dependencies |
| The Outer Sterling Area: | Bolivia |
| British Colonial Empire | Colombia |
| Australia | Costa Rica |
| New Zealand | Cuba |
| India | Dominican Republic |
| Ceylon | El Salvador |
| Pakistan | Ecuador |
| Burma | Guatemala |
| Eire | Haiti |
| Iceland | Honduras |
| Iraq | Mexico |
| Jordan | Nicaragua |
| Libya | *Panama |
| South Africa | *Philippine Republic |
| | Venezuela |

*The currencies of Norway, Sweden and Denmark may be accepted in settlement by Sterling Area residents but there is no requirement that they must be offered for sale to an authorized dealer. The currencies of the other countries marked with an asterisk are the so-called 'specified' currencies: these also may be accepted in settlement but must be offered for sale to an authorized dealer.

[1] So far as earnings from exports are concerned, the control is entirely unrestrictive, and is intended solely to ensure that foreign currencies earned (other than the three Scandinavian currencies) are duly surrendered.

| *Transferable Account Countries* | *'Bilateral' Countries*[1] |
|---|---|
| Austria | *Argentina |
| Chile | *Belgian Monetary Area |
| Czechoslovakia | *Brazil |
| *Danish Monetary Area | Bulgaria |
| Egypt | *Canada |
| Ethiopia | China |
| Finland | Formosa |
| Greece | *French Monetary Area |
| Italian Monetary Area | Hungary |
| *Netherlands Monetary Area | Iran |
| *Norway | Israel |
| Poland | Japan |
| Spanish Monetary Area | *Lebanon |
| Sudan | Paraguay |
| *Sweden | Peru |
| Thailand | *Portuguese Monetary Area |
| U.S.S.R. | Roumania |
| Western Germany | *Switzerland |
| | *Syria |
| | Tangier |
| | Turkey |
| | *Uruguay |
| | Vatican City |
| | Yugoslavia |

American Account the Sterling Area controls place no restriction whatever on its transfer to any countries other than those on the 'bilateral' list in Table 11. Transfers to 'bilateral' countries are subject to administrative approval but are allowed liberally. The British authorities will on demand always convert American Account sterling into U.S. dollars.

*Transferable Account Countries.* Sterling on Transferable Account is not convertible into U.S. dollars or any other currency. However Transferable Account sterling enjoys

*See note on p. 136.

[1]Despite the label 'bilateral', these countries may in many cases receive sterling from, and pay sterling to, other bilateral countries or Transferable Account countries, on a basis of 'administrative transferability'.

automatic transferability for *current* payments to other Transferable Account countries and to the remaining members of the 'small residual group'[1] and is accepted for all payments to the Sterling Area. The use made of sterling by the Transferable Account countries, other than for making payments to the Sterling Area, is very considerable, as will be seen from Table 12.

*Bilateral Countries.* The present position is that, except in the case of Canada and Argentina, Bilateral Account sterling is not convertible into gold or dollars.[2] Bilateral Account sterling is accepted for all payments to the Sterling Area, but for payments outside this Area it enjoys only administrative transferability. It should be noted however that the facilities for administrative transferability are widely used, as is shown by the figures in Table 12.

## TABLE 12[3]

TRANSFERS OF STERLING

*between Countries outside the Sterling and American Account Areas (£ millions)*

| | *1948* | *1949* |
|---|---|---|
| Under Automatic Facilities .. .. | 88 | 144 |
| Under Administrative Facilities .. | 152 | 124 |
| | 240 | 268 |

None of the above remarks applies to blocked sterling. The estimated total of all sterling balances as at the end of

[1]See footnote 3, p. 132. Two former members of the 'small residual group', namely Cyrenaica and Tripolitania, are now united as the United Kingdom of Libya, which joined the Sterling Area in January 1952.

[2]Until the formation of the E.P.U. in 1949 Belgium, Portugal, Switzerland and certain other European 'bilateral' countries undertook to accumulate sterling only up to a limited swing, beyond which settlement in gold or dollars was required. It might therefore be said that in the appropriate circumstances sterling acquired by these countries was convertible. However, these conversion arrangements were terminated when the E.P.U. came into force.

[3]Taken from the Bank of England's *Report* for the year ended 28th February, 1950, p. 10.

1949 was rather over £3.3 billions, of which about £1.3 billions were blocked by agreement with the holders. Details are given in Table 13, and it will be seen that much the largest holdings of blocked sterling were, in descending order of magnitude, those of India, Egypt, Pakistan and Iraq. Blocked sterling is largely invested in British Treasury Bills, yielding less than one per cent per annum interest, and may not be converted into gold or dollars or paid to any other country so long as it remains blocked. Until recently, all the blocking was on a short-term basis, the relevant agreements needing to be re-negotiated at intervals of a year or so, but the Colombo Plan of October 1950[1] laid down a long term programme for the release of part of the blocked sterling held by India, Pakistan and Ceylon, and early in 1951 similar arrangements were made with Egypt and Israel.

The rate of release of blocked sterling has been generous (many would say unduly generous[2]); £5 million were released in 1946, £156½ million in 1947, £267 million in 1948 and £218 million in 1949, compared 'with the annual release of £43 million tentatively anticipated as a reasonable rate of release at the time of the Washington loan agreement'.[3]

The programmes of future releases to India, Pakistan, Ceylon and Egypt have also been subject to criticism, partly because no provision has been made for cancelling any of the balances, partly because the annual rate of release represents an 'excessive' burden on Britain's balance of payments.

The factor which prevented sterling from resuming at the end of the war its pre-war role of an international currency, universally acceptable in settlement of international accounts, was the persistence of serious international disequilibria (to be described in the next chapter), which led Britain to maintain restrictions on the transferability of sterling to hard currency countries. Only for a short period, in the first half of 1947, were these restrictions relaxed, and then they had to be hastily reimposed.

[1]Cmd. 8080.

[2]See the note on 'Boosting Unrequited Exports' in the *Economist*, 13th August, 1949, p. 368.

[3]*Economist*, 5th November, 1949, p. 1023 and 13th May, 1950, p. 1076.

## TABLE 13[1]

ESTIMATED STERLING BALANCES OF OTHER COUNTRIES AT THE END OF 1949

*(in £ million)*

| Country | Total | Blocked |
|---|---|---|
| *Sterling Area Countries* | | |
| Australia .. .. | 375 | — |
| New Zealand .. .. | 60 | — |
| South Africa .. .. | 55 | — |
| Eire .. .. .. | 225 | — |
| India .. .. .. | 720[2] | 680 |
| Pakistan .. .. .. | 140[2] | 130 |
| Iraq .. .. .. | 82 | 82 |
| Ceylon .. .. .. | 45 | 40 |
| Colonial Empire .. | 620 | 25 |
| *Other Countries* | | |
| Egypt .. .. .. | 322 | 253 |
| Palestine .. .. .. | 30 | — |
| European Countries .. | 381 | 25 |
| Latin America .. .. | 88 | 51 |
| Others .. .. .. | 112 | — |
| *Unidentified, Errors and Omissions* .. .. .. | 89 | 64 |
| GRAND TOTAL .. | 3,344 | 1,350 |

Yet, even in the absence of full transferability, sterling enjoys great popularity as a means of international payment. It has for example been officially estimated that in 1948 no less than £5 billions of goods were traded internationally against sterling, compared with a total international trade in goods of £13.8 billions. Statistics for other international pay-

[1]From the *Banker*, May 1950, and the *Economist*, 13th May, 1950, pp. 1075–7.

[2]Includes some £175 millions hypothecated to cover pension obligations.

ments are not available, but it is believed that probably more than 50 per cent of all international payments were made in sterling.

*The Pathology of Sterling*

The powers which the monetary authorities of a country are able to exercise over transactions in that country's currency are in practice severely limited, and any currency which is subject to exchange controls is almost sure to provide examples of 'leaks' and of 'black' or 'cheap' exchange rates. Sterling is far from being an exception to this rule, for though the exchange controls of the Sterling Area are of great technical competence, their task is considerably complicated by the widespread use of sterling as an international currency. It is therefore instructive to consider the weaknesses which appear in the sterling arrangements just described, whenever they are subject to pressure, as they were, for example, in the middle of 1949.

All exchange controls, even those in countries whose currencies are not used outside their own frontiers, are liable to leaks in the form of unauthorized transactions by residents in the home country. Such transactions usually comprise the use of the proceeds of exports to finance unauthorized imports or unauthorized transfers of capital to another country. Unauthorized imports of commodities can be made difficult by an efficient customs service, and unauthorized 'invisible' imports (for example holidays abroad), though less easy to stop, cannot give rise to more than a minor leak. Unauthorized transfers of capital are however a much more serious matter, since the desire to make such transfers may in certain circumstances[1] be widespread, and exporters may well be able to evade the control either by understating the value of their exports or by giving extended credit to their foreign customers.

As an example of the former kind of evasion we can suppose that Mr. A, an English exporter, expected in the middle of 1949 that sterling was about to be devalued in relation to the U.S. dollar and therefore considered it in his interest to hold as much of his capital as possible in dollars rather than in

[1]As for instance in mid-1949, when a devaluation of sterling was widely expected.

sterling. Prevented by the exchange control from transferring his capital simply by buying dollars for sterling, he decided to transfer $200,000 illegally by undervaluing his next consignment of exports to an American customer, Mr. B. The price B was prepared to pay for the consignment was $1,000,000, but A incorrectly declared to the British exchange control and customs authorities that B would be paying only $800,000. Payment was then effected by B openly paying A $800,000 (which A had immediately to surrender to the British authorities in exchange for sterling) and secretly paying a further $200,000 into an American bank deposit held by a nominee of A.

The kind of evasion illustrated by the above example is in practice extremely difficult to detect, except where the undervaluation of the exports is so serious as to attract the attention of the customs officials. Another characteristic of this type of evasion is that it does not give rise to a 'black' exchange rate, since A's illegal holding of dollars was never exchanged for sterling. We can however imagine a more complicated transaction in which A makes a practice of transferring his capital to America (by undervaluing his exports) and repatriating it illegally by selling his dollars for sterling, not however to the British authorities at the official rate (£1=$4 in mid-1949), but instead to another Englishman, Mr. C, who so wishes to transfer his capital to America that he is prepared to buy A's dollars at a 'black' rate of (say) £1=$3. Such transactions undoubtedly occur in practice, but are much more likely to be detected than in cases where the exporter attempts merely to transfer his own capital, simply because more people are involved in the illegal act.[1]

The other device available to Mr. A for transferring capital abroad is the granting of extended trade credit. It is of course normal commercial practice for exporters to sell on credit to their foreign customers, and the most that an exchange control can reasonably attempt to do is to set an upper limit (six months, or some such period) to the term of credit that an exporter may allow. If therefore our exporter, Mr. A, likes to hold a promise of dollars from B in preference to holding

[1]The parties to the offence would be at least the exporter A and the investor C, but there would very probably be a go-between as well.

sterling, he will grant B at least the full permitted term of credit and may then attempt to extend it further on one pretext or another; and since there are perfectly legitimate reasons why a foreign customer might need to delay payment, it is virtually impossible for the British control to take action against any but the most flagrant cases of procrastination.

Experience in the post-war years has shown that no exchange control can prevent very considerable capital movements in the form of variations in international trade credit. If for example a particular country's currency is distrusted, a transfer of capital out of the suspect country occurs both as the result of an extension of trade credit by the country's exporters and also because imports are paid for as promptly as possible. A considerable part of the drain of gold and dollars from Britain in the months prior to the devaluation of sterling in September 1949 was undoubtedly caused by the need to accommodate an increase in export credit granted, and a reduction in import credit accepted, by British traders.

Another leak in the British exchange control, which also arises through British residents breaking British law, is the export of British bank-notes. To facilitate its work in supervising international payments in sterling, the British exchange control has tried to stop the use of British bank-notes overseas. In particular, tourists are permitted to take out only £5 per head in notes, and then only for meeting immediate out of pocket expenses on their return to this country. Unscrupulous tourists have however made a practice of spending abroad their £5 in notes and even of taking out extra notes for this purpose. Such notes are readily bought by foreigners wishing to pay their travelling and other expenses in Britain, but usually at an appreciable discount, since in order to bring in more than £5 in notes the holders have to smuggle them through the British customs. Dealings in British bank-notes are conducted in organized markets in various Continental centres, especially Zurich, and financial newspapers regularly report from these centres the 'black' rates for sterling bank-notes against other currencies.

Let us now turn to those leaks in the sterling control arrangements which arise from the use of sterling as an international currency. These leaks have been serious on occasions (e.g. mid-1949) and are difficult to prevent. Indeed Britain is unusual in both practising exchange control and at the same time attempting to promote the international use of her currency; most countries with exchange controls have thought it desirable to prevent the international use of their currencies, for example by requiring their exporters to exact payment in foreign currencies. (British exports can of course *always* be paid for in sterling.)

The most serious 'foreign' leak in the sterling control arrangements occurs when the monetary authorities in a foreign country either refuse to stabilize the price of sterling by buying and selling it freely against the local currency, or when alternatively they do stabilize the price of sterling, but at a level which gives rise to a disorderly cross rate between sterling and a hard currency, particularly the U.S. dollar. The effect of disorderly cross rates between sterling and the dollar has already been considered in Chapter VI in connection with the currency practices of Italy before November 1948 and of France between February 1948 and September 1949.[1] There we saw that the result of 'cheap' sterling[2] in Italy and France was to divert trade in such a way that these countries obtained dollars which would otherwise have gone into the Sterling Area dollar pool. A similar result would be likely to occur if any other country's monetary authorities failed to stabilize the price of sterling, in terms of the local currency, at the appropriate level. In practice most countries have agreed to avoid disorderly cross rates in sterling, but there still remains a number of smaller countries (e.g. Siam, Syria, and the Lebanon) where although there may be an official rate of exchange for certain governmental transactions, the local price of sterling bought by importers is simply allowed to find its own level in a free market, which has usually meant that sterling has been 'cheap' in relation to the dollar.

It will be recalled that one way in which a disorderly

[1]Above, p. 71.

[2]This 'cheap' sterling was not 'black' sterling, since none of the transactions which led to the purchase or sale of sterling at a cheap price in relation to dollars were in contravention of any country's laws or regulations.

sterling-dollar cross rate causes a loss of dollars to the Sterling Area dollar pool is that it encourages merchants to buy goods in the Sterling Area for indirect export (via a third country, and possibly after processing) to the United States. A similar diversion of trade may arise for other reasons, of which two have been from time to time (e.g. in mid-1949) of considerable importance in practice.

*First*, foreign holders of sterling may (no less than British holders) decide that it would be to their advantage to hold dollars instead—because, for instance, they expect that sterling is shortly to be devalued in relation to the dollar. In these circumstances the discontented foreign holders of sterling can achieve their object either by themselves buying Sterling Area goods with their sterling and reselling them in America for dollars, or alternatively by selling their sterling at a discount to a merchant who would undertake the same transaction. What exactly the latter alternative involves can be made clear by a hypothetical example. Mr. X, a Ruritanian resident, has a holding of £100,000 of Transferable Account sterling (Ruritania being a Transferable Account country) which he wishes to convert into dollars. This holding he makes over to a merchant, Mr. Y, at a cheap rate of (say) £1=$3, the official rate at the time being £1=$4. Y uses the £100,000 to buy Sterling Area goods which he then resells in America for something more than $300,000—let us say for $400,000. Of this amount, $300,000 is paid into an American bank deposit in X's name (in this way X is paid for his sterling) and the remaining $100,000 is available to cover expenses and as profit for Y.

*Second*, it can be shown that merchants importing goods into countries outside both the American Account Area and the Sterling Area may well find it to their advantage to exchange sterling for dollars at a black rate, whenever the sterling prices of commodities are higher (at the prevailing official rate of exchange) than the dollar prices of the same goods, or when certain commodities cannot be bought for sterling at all. Such a state of affairs has obtained from time to time since the end of the war: for example in the middle of 1949 the sterling prices of many primary commodities were appreciably higher than the corresponding dollar prices,[1] while many luxury goods, produced mainly in the United States, could hardly be bought for sterling at all. The kind of transactions which occurred at this time, and caused a leak in the sterling exchange control, can be illustrated by a variant of our previous story about Mr. Y.

In our new version, we abandon our Mr. X, the Ruritanian holder of sterling, and replace him by a Mr. Z, a Ruritanian importer. Mr. Z, to pay for many of the goods he imports, needs either sterling or dollars, which he can obtain at the official rates of exchange from the Ruritanian monetary authorities. Unfortunately for him, however, he is allowed only a very limited ration of dollars for the purchase of 'non-essential' goods or of goods which can be obtained for sterling. If only he could obtain more dollars he could make larger profits, for he could then import from the United States more of the goods which are relatively expensive, or even unobtainable, from sterling sources. The Ruritanian authorities are however prepared to make a concession. Their general rule is that if a Ruritanian obtains dollars (for example, by exporting goods to the United States) he must sell them to the authorities at the official exchange rate, but if Z, or any other Ruritanian, obtains *extra* dollars for his country, he may use them himself for buying extra imports. This is where Y comes in. He can obtain extra dollars by the indirect export of Sterling Area goods to the United States, and these dollars he is prepared to sell to Z for sterling at a black rate, just as he was prepared in our previous example to sell them to X.

It may be wondered why, if merchants such as Y can obtain black market sterling in this way, they should ever buy sterling at the official price. Why indeed do such merchants not bid exclusively for black market sterling until its price is forced up to a level not much lower than the official price? The answer to this question is that Y, in arranging the indirect export of Sterling Area goods to the United States, incurs expenses and runs risks which could be avoided if the goods were shipped directly to the United States and the dollar proceeds exchanged for sterling at the official rate. In the first

[1]See below, p. 170.

place, Y incurs extra shipping expenses. Instead of shipping (say) Australian wool direct to the United States, he has to conceal its destination from the Sterling Area authorities by sending it first to (say) Holland and again from there to its final destination. Second, if Y is himself a Ruritanian, it is doubtful whether the Ruritanian authorities would willingly permit Y to sell dollars to X (so that X could transfer his capital to the United States) instead of selling them to the authorities at the official exchange rate. Hence an evasion of the Ruritanian exchange regulations might be necessary. (The Ruritanian authorities might not however object to Y selling his dollars to Z, whose transactions would supply more scarce goods to the Ruritanian market, without depleting Ruritania's official dollar reserve.)

If on the other hand Y is not a Ruritanian, means must be found to make a transfer of sterling to Y from X or Z, even though the British exchange control does not authorize sterling to be drawn from Transferable Accounts for purposes of buying dollars. If Y lives in a second Transferable Account country, it may be fairly easy to transfer the sterling to him under cover of a fictitious purchase of *goods* from him, and the same deception might be practised successfully, under the British exchange control's 'administrative transferability' arrangements, if Y resided in one of the 'bilateral' countries. But if Y is an American, he could get Ruritanian sterling transferred to him only by working through an agent resident outside the American Account Area, preferably in one of the Transferable Account countries. It is thus easy to see that in almost all circumstances our merchant Y is involved in considerable expense and risk, and in consequence will buy X's and Z's sterling for dollars only if it is offered at an attractive discount. The relatively poor price which Transferable Account and Bilateral sterling will fetch on the black market reduces the leak of dollars from the Sterling Area pool to fairly insignificant proportions save in exceptional circumstances. There is however always at least a trickle of transactions through the black market, and at certain international financial centres, such as New York, Zurich and Tangiers, intermediaries are always prepared to quote buying and selling prices for Transferable Account sterling, French sterling, Argentine sterling, and so on.

It is sometimes argued that black market quotations necessarily reflect the 'true' value of sterling in terms of other currencies, and that the corresponding official exchange rates ought to be brought into conformity with them. There is however no justification for this view: though the official exchange rates may be, in a sense, 'artificially' sustained by exchange control regulations, it is equally true that black market rates are 'artificially' depressed by the trouble and expense involved in evading these regulations. Neither the official rates nor the black rates indicate what the *laissez-faire* rates would be, in the absence of official intervention.

This short story of the pathology of sterling is very far from being exhaustive, but sketchy though it is, it may serve to give the reader a better sense of perspective on what can, and what cannot, be achieved by exchange controls.

# *PART THREE*

# *THE COURSE OF EVENTS SINCE THE WAR*

## CHAPTER X

## BEFORE SEPTEMBER 1949

THE flood of devaluations released by the devaluation of sterling in September 1949 marked a turning point in international monetary history. The period from the end of hostilities up to September 1949 was characterized by a considerable degree of historical unity, partly because the major international disequilibria of the period arose from the war and from economic problems directly attributable to the war, partly because there was no widespread attempt in the period to deal with these disequilibria by means of adjustments to exchange rates. The devaluations of September 1949 not only represented an abrupt break with the previous tradition of exchange stability, but also partially liquidated the disequilibria of the preceding period. The Korean War, which followed in June 1950, completed, if only temporarily, the liquidation of these disequilibria. It therefore seems appropriate to treat the period prior to September 1949 separately from the succeeding period, and to distinguish it by giving it the title of 'the post-war period'.

*Exchange Rates*

Though the post-war period, thus defined, was characterized by remarkably stable exchange rates, this stability was achieved only by the use of exchange controls, which sometimes led to disorderly cross rates and (particularly in South America) to multiple currency practices. This state of affairs, as the B.I.S. points out in its nineteenth *Annual Report*,[1] was in marked contrast to what happened after the war of 1914–18:

> After the first world war, it took more than five years before any European currency was formally "stabilised", which at that time meant linked to gold again at the par rate. Before stabilisation took place, the various currencies were subject to sometimes rather wild, sometimes quite moderate, fluctuations; but for each currency there was not more than one rate quoted (apart from a slight spread between buying and selling rates) and the various currencies could be bought and sold freely for all purposes at the rates thus quoted in the respective exchange markets. In order to steady quotations, central banks (and sometimes governments also) had at times to support their currencies by entering the market as purchasers or had to buy up any offer of foreign currencies which might threaten to raise the value of the national currency more than was desired, those being the early days of the gold exchange standard. . . .
>
> Since the second world war, the exchange system has been of a different kind. "Par rates" have been fixed for most currencies and at those rates current commercial and other transactions have to be settled, the settlements taking place largely through clearing and other bilateral accounts without any specific transactions in the open exchange markets. Not only capital transfers but current operations, whether commercial or financial, are, in most countries, dependent upon an "allotment of foreign exchange" by the official Control. This being so, there are normally no fluctuations in the official rates. Any alterations (beyond such minor modifications of a fractional nature as the authorities may decide upon from time to time) are, under the new system, made on the basis of official decisions applicable from certain definite dates (as was the case in July 1946 when the Canadian dollar was appreciated by 10 per cent and the Swedish crown by 16.6 per cent). Thus, the official par rates are in no immediate way dependent upon quotations in actual exchange markets. . . .

Though the general picture prior to September 1949 was one of stability, there are a number of events to record. *First*, the main ex-enemy countries, China, and several eastern European countries, entered upon the peace with their economies in a highly inflationary condition and the value of their

[1]See the *Report*, p. 118.

currencies steadily falling. Apart from China, all of these countries had restored stability before September 1949. In particular, Greece, Hungary and Poland stabilized their currencies in 1946, Roumania and Italy followed suit in 1947, Germany introduced a completely new currency, the Deutsche Mark, in June 1948, and Japan stabilized the yen in April 1949. *Second*, there were three cases of currencies being appreciated in relation to the U.S. dollar—namely the Canadian dollar and the Swedish crown in July 1946 (respectively by 10 and 16.6 per cent) and the New Zealand pound in August 1948 (by 24 per cent). In all three cases the main purpose was to combat excess demand in the home market.[1] *Third*, there were a small number of deliberate depreciations of wholly or partly stabilized currencies, notably by Turkey in 1946, and by Mexico and France in 1948 and 1949.

The most important examples of disorderly cross rates in the period we are considering were those which prevailed in Italy up to November 1948 and in France between February 1948 and September 1949. Both of these cases have been mentioned already in Chapter VI. The resort to multiple currency practices was more widespread, as will be seen from the following list[2] of countries engaging in such practices:

COUNTRIES WITH MULTIPLE EXCHANGE RATES IN THE POST-WAR PERIOD

| *Latin America* | *Elsewhere* |
|---|---|
| Argentina | Spain |
| Bolivia | Iran |
| Brazil | Lebanon |
| Chile | Syria |
| Colombia | Thailand |
| Costa Rica | |
| Ecuador | |
| Nicaragua | |
| Paraguay | |
| Peru | |
| Uruguay | |
| Venezuela | |

[1]See above, p. 65.
[2]Assembled from various I.M.F. publications.

### *The Causes of the Post-war Disequilibria*

The chief cause of the major post-war disequilibria, and particularly of the so-called dollar gap, was the devastation of Europe and of certain other countries, including the important dollar-earning regions of Malaya and the East Indies. Not only was there actual destruction of material assets, but maintenance work and the replacement of worn-out and obsolete equipment was postponed; moreover, a great deal of manufacturing industry became highly specialized for the production of munitions and other requirements of war. This last factor was particularly important in the case of the United Kingdom, whose contribution to the war effort required her to direct her economy away from exports and civilian requirements and to rely on Lend-Lease imports for goods which had previously been either made at home or obtained from overseas in exchange for British exports.[1]

The return of peace brought further causes of disequilibria, which served particularly to aggravate Europe's need for dollars. The European harvests of 1946 and 1947 were very poor, owing to unfavourable weather, and the hard winter of early 1947 was partially responsible for the British coal crisis. The establishment of an Iron Curtain, through which trade passed only with great difficulty, between the complementary economies of eastern and western Europe, had the effect of delaying reconstruction and industrialization in the East and of making the West more dependent than before on non-European sources of supply for foodstuffs and raw materials.[2] The division of Germany was a special case of this malady: western Germany, whose population was increased by 10 million refugees and displaced persons, was cut off both from its former granary in eastern Germany and from its pre-war markets behind the Iron Curtain.[3]

The fortunes of industry and agriculture in the American

[1]See *Statistical Material Presented during the Washington Negotiations*, published by H.M.S.O., 1945, Cmd. 6707.

[2]See 'The Problem of East-West Trade' in the *Economic Survey of Europe in 1949*, p. 91.

[3]See the article on 'Pre-war Regional Interdependence and Post-war Interzonal Trade in Germany', in the E.C.E.'s *Economic Bulletin for Europe*, Vol. 1, No. 3.

continent during and immediately after the war, and especially in the United States, were in marked contrast to what happened in Europe. Nowhere in the former continent was productive capacity impaired by the war, and in the U.S.A. there was a vast increase in industrial output, with little or no decline in the production of civilian goods, a great increase in agricultural acreage, and a remarkable series of good harvests. Hence the goods which Europe so urgently needed, and which she could not produce for herself, were available from across the Atlantic, and the only problem was to find means to pay for them. Had the American continent shared the misfortunes of Europe there would not have been so intractable a settlement problem, because such a problem arises only when there are goods to be bought; but on the other hand there would have been immeasurably more hardship in Europe. Rough measures of the decline in industrial and agricultural output in western Europe, which had occurred by the end of the war, are provided by the indices shown in Table 14. These indices also show the extent of the subsequent recovery.

## TABLE 14

INDICES OF INDUSTRIAL AND AGRICULTURAL PRODUCTION IN EUROPE[1]

Industrial Production:

| *1938* | *1946* | *1947* | *1948* | *1949* | *1950* |
|---|---|---|---|---|---|
| 100 | 72 | 82 | 96 | 109 | 124 |

Agricultural Production:

| *1934–38* | *1946–47* | *1947–48* | *1948–49* | *1949–50* |
|---|---|---|---|---|
| 100 | 81 | 80 | 91 | 94 |

Another factor which contributed to the post-war international disequilibria was the change in the pattern of international indebtedness brought about by the war. In the early stages of the war, before the advent of Lend-Lease, Britain and her European allies, but particularly Britain herself, were forced to realize a large amount of their overseas investments in order to finance their imports. Moreover, the rise in prices which occurred during the war greatly reduced the purchasing

[1]Calculated by the E.C.E.

power of the income from the investments which remained. In Britain's case she had to realize about £1 billion of her overseas assets, and in addition she acquired about £3 billion of new indebtedness in the form of accumulations of sterling by other countries. Measured in the overseas goods which it can command, Britain's net income from overseas investments has declined to about one third of its pre-war amount.

The disequilibria of the post-war years are attributable not only to the war itself but also to its economic aftermath, and in particular to inflation. In the immediate post-war years, conditions of excess demand were virtually general throughout the world. A United Nations' survey comments thus:[1]

> A major factor in the world-wide inflationary pressures was the existence of demand for consumption goods pent up during the war. In many instances this pent-up demand was supported by accumulated holdings of liquid assets. In the devastated countries and in some under-developed areas of the world an even more important factor was the decline in *per capita* consumer supplies, especially of food, through reductions in agricultural output, declines in industrial productivity, and in some cases increases in population.

In many countries these inflationary tendencies were reflected in 'open' inflation, with rapidly rising prices. In other cases the inflation was 'suppressed' by the use of price controls and rationing.

The effect of open inflation in any country, X, is that the rise in the prices of home-produced goods tends to divert demand to imported goods, and thus to increase external payments, unless special steps are taken (e.g. increased trade and currency restrictions or currency depreciation) to counteract this tendency. At the same time the rise in prices in X will, unless offset by currency depreciation, make export goods produced by X cost more to foreign customers. This will tend to reduce the quantity bought by foreigners; and as a result X's total earnings from exports will either fall or increase depending on the elasticity of foreign demand. On balance the effect of

[1]*Inflationary and Deflationary Tendencies* 1946–1948, published in June 1949, p. 3.

open inflation on X's balance of current payments is likely to be unfavourable, unless X adopts currency depreciation or other offsetting measures.[1]

The open inflations which occurred after the First World War were all associated with rapid currency depreciation and may therefore not have had the effect of worsening the balance of payments of the countries concerned. In the more recent post-war period, however, the countries suffering inflation maintained their exchange rates and admitted imports to the extent permitted by their available supplies of liquidity, for they had come to realize that any reduction in the availability of imports, and any diversion of goods to export markets, would have the effect of reducing the supplies of goods on which the excessive home demand could be expended, thus aggravating the inflationary pressure. In these circumstances, open inflation tended to have an adverse effect on a country's balance of current payments.

In the case of a country with suppressed inflation, the excess of demand over supply is not permitted to lead to a rise in prices, which are held down by price controls.[2] Instead, the excess demand is held back by rationing and by shortages, but unless rationing is very strict (stricter than in practice it ever is) any increase in the pressure of demand tends to stimulate imports (since imported goods find a ready market) and to divert to customers at home the supplies that would normally be available for export.

Thus in the conditions prevailing after the war of 1939–45, inflation, whether open or suppressed, almost invariably had the effect of worsening a country's balance of current payments, and the countries which mastered their inflations first tended to develop external surpluses, while those where inflation remained longest had deficits. Hence the chronology of the control of inflation is important to an understanding of the international disequilibria of the post-war world. The following quotations from various official reports give an outline of what happened:

[1]See above p. 49, footnote 1.

[2]Sometimes the price controls are informal: thus a government may 'advise' a manufacturers' association to restrain the increase in the prices of its members' products.

In 1948, the inflationary patterns of the preceding two years were still prevalent in a large part of the world. Nevertheless there was some tendency for the relaxation of the inflationary pressures. The pressure of pent-up demand weakened in many countries. There was also some increase in the supplies of consumption goods *per capita* and considerable easing of specific shortages. The supply of food generally improved towards the end of the year after the favourable harvests of 1948. The full anti-inflationary impact of this factor, however, could not be felt until 1949.

For the first time since the end of the war, there appeared in 1948 and early 1949 some deflationary tendencies, in the form of actual slackening in economic activity or appearance of factors foreshadowing such slackening. Italy, which suffers from considerable chronic unemployment, experienced in addition a recession which began in the autumn of 1947. It was followed by a recovery in the second half of 1948, and another set-back in early 1949. There was also a considerable rise in unemployment in Belgium in the course of 1948. Finally, there was some involuntary accumulation of inventories in the United States in 1948, and unemployment increased significantly at the beginning of 1949.[1]

Hence it would appear that, apart from a temporary recession in Italy in 1947, the first signs of the end of inflation appeared in 1948 in Belgium and the United States.

'In the first half of 1949, inflationary pressures continued to weaken throughout the world'.[2] By the middle of the year deflation, rather than inflation, had become a problem in the United States, and in western Europe the same could be said of Belgium and to a lesser extent of Western Germany, Italy and Switzerland. Indeed, of the larger O.E.E.C. countries, only the United Kingdom, Scandinavia and the Netherlands could be said o be still subject to inflationary pressures.[3]

In other parts of the world the subsidence of inflation in 1949 was uneven. In Latin America, 'anti-inflationary factors

[1]Both quotations are from *Inflationary and Deflationary Tendencies*, p. 4.

[2]United Nations: *Recent Developments in the World Economic Situation*, published October 1949, p. 4.

[3]For the history of the progress of deflation in Western Europe, and of the causes thereof, see the O.E.E.C.'s *Report on Internal Financial Stability*, published in October 1949, pp. 15 to 20. Also see the E.C.E.'s *Economic Survey of Europe in* 1949, Chapter 3.

were significant'[1] in four of the smaller American Account countries, namely 'Cuba and Venezuela and, to a lesser extent, in Mexico and Colombia', but outside the American Account Area inflation continued: 'inflationary elements were still active in Argentina, Brazil, Paraguay, Peru and Uruguay'. 'In Asia and the Far East [but not in China] inflationary pressures also diminished towards the end of 1948 and early in 1949, largely as a result of an increase in the food supply'.

In the light of the preceding description of the causes of the post-war disequilibria, we should expect a strong tendency for there to be flows of settlements in the direction of certain countries and groups of countries, namely:

1. The whole American continent, but particularly the U.S.A. and Canada, where inflationary pressure was never so pronounced as in Latin America.
2. The former neutral countries, or at any rate those neutrals (particularly Switzerland, Portugal and Sweden) which had efficient governments, capable of taking measures to moderate inflation.
3. The first ex-belligerents to master inflation, namely the United States, Belgium, Italy and Western Germany.

The tendency for settlements to flow towards these countries might be expected either to show itself openly, in the form of settlements actually effected, or alternatively to be suppressed, whether by unemployment in the rest of the world or by trade and payments restrictions. To what extent did these various symptoms appear in practice?

### *Suppressed and Open Disequilibria in the Post-war Period*

So far as suppressed disequilibria are concerned, there is little evidence in the post-war period of suppression by unemployment. As we have seen, the only countries which may have suffered from inadequate demand in this period were the United States, Switzerland, Belgium, Western Germany and Italy. In the first two of these cases, the trouble coincided with an external surplus, which suggests that the inadequacy

[1]The quotations in this paragraph are from *Recent Developments in the World Economic Situation*, p. 10.

of demand was not related to any need to suppress an external deficit. Hence there remain only three possible cases of the suppression of disequilibria by means of unemployment, and even then there is no clear evidence that the emergence of unemployment was due to balance-of-payments difficulties.

Though unemployment was rare in the post-war period, the other symptoms of suppressed disequilibria—restrictions on trade and payments—were endemic, and it is safe to conclude that many were imposed specifically to suppress flows of settlements which would otherwise have exhausted the paying country's liquidity. Such a conclusion can be safely drawn in the case of discriminating restrictions,[1] which were in widespread and continuous use against the United States and the other American Account countries, Canada, Switzerland, and Belgium and in occasional use against various other countries (for example Germany).

In the case of non-discriminatory restrictions the evidence is much more difficult to interpret, since such restrictions may be imposed for so many reasons other than the suppression of disequilibria. Our task is however made somewhat easier by the widespread, though admittedly far from universal, tendency in the post-war period for countries to deal with external disequilibria by means of restrictions enforced by exchange control—other restrictions, such as tariffs, being reserved mainly for other purposes.[2] On this basis it would seem that the only countries which did not impose restrictions for suppressing disequilibria were the United States and many of the other American Account countries, Canada, Switzerland, and Belgium.[3] The evidence of restrictions, for what it is worth, thus points to these countries as being those to which settlements tended to flow so strongly as to call for suppressive action by the rest of the world.

The remarkable feature of the post-war period was however the size of the open disequilibria which persisted, despite the drastic measures which were taken to suppress them. The

[1]See above, p. 60, footnote 2.

[2]There is no strong economic foundation for this distinction, since the two classes of restrictions can be made to produce almost identical results. See above, pp. 27–29.

[3]I.M.F.'s *First Annual Report on Exchange Restrictions*, pp. 22–6.

available balance-of-payments statistics are so unsatisfactory that the total of the open disequilibria in the period cannot be estimated very accurately, but the overall surplus of the United States alone is known to have been in the region of $30 billions, and it is doubtful whether all the other overall surpluses taken together would add more than 10 per cent to this total. On this basis the total overall surpluses in the post-war period would be some $33 billions, a truly enormous amount, and—more remarkable still—a single country accounted for almost the whole of it.

The second largest surplus country was Canada, with an overall surplus of about $1 billion. A few members of the Sterling Area had surpluses, but the Area as a whole was in deficit with the rest of the world. A number of Latin American countries also had surpluses, among them Argentina and Venezuela. In Europe probably only Switzerland had an overall surplus, taking the post-war period as a whole.

The main overall deficits which balanced these overall surpluses were as follows, the figures quoted being highly approximate:

1. The O.E.E.C. countries, other than the U.K. and Switzerland, together with their dependent colonial territories,—about $20 billions.
2. The United Kingdom,—about $5 billions.
3. The outer Sterling Area,—about $2 billions.
4. The United States' Pacific protégés: China, Japan and the Philippines,—about $4 billions.

*International Settlements in the Post-war Period*

If however we wish to understand the pattern of international settlements in the post-war period, it is not sufficient to look simply at the overall surpluses and deficits which prevailed. We also need information about bilateral relationships—preferably in the form of a table, like Table 3 on page 41, showing all the bilateral deficits of all the countries of the world, with closed circuits of deficits eliminated and the various countries ranged in order of their 'strength'. Unfortunately the compilation of such a table—Table *X*, let us call it—is at present quite impossible, owing to the inadequacies of available statistics: all we can do is to try to establish very roughly the order in which the various countries, or groups of countries, might be expected to appear.

Our first task is to settle whether any country was stronger than the United States—the country with the largest overall surplus. Of the countries with overall surpluses, only one—Switzerland—seems to be able to claim a bilateral surplus with the United States: this evidence therefore points to Switzerland as being the strongest country, followed by the United States. Next to the United States, in an order which we cannot satisfactorily guess, would be a group—the 'Intermediate Group', let us call it—comprising the remaining surplus countries and those deficit countries[1] whose only appreciable bilateral deficits were with the surplus countries. This group would include Canada and most of the Latin American countries. Belgium would also be included, but otherwise it is doubtful whether any other western European country would fall within this group, taking the post-war period as a whole. After the Intermediate Group of countries in Table *X* would be countries which ran appreciable bilateral deficits not only with the surplus countries but also with other deficit countries. This 'Weak Group' of countries would be very extensive, and would range from those whose bilateral deficits were solely with Switzerland, the U.S.A. and our Intermediate Group of countries to the (unidentifiable) weakest country. The most important members of Weak Group would be the Sterling Area and almost all the European countries except Switzerland and Belgium.

The order in which we have placed countries in our imaginary Table *X* throws considerable light on the hierarchy of currencies in the post-war period. The strongest country, Switzerland, was prepared to accumulate gold and the currencies of certain other countries in strictly limited amounts, but otherwise she required settlement in her own currency, Swiss francs, of which however there were only very limited holdings outside Switzerland after the war. It soon appeared that the total means available to the rest of the world for

[1]The label 'surplus (or deficit) country' refers of course to a country with an *overall* surplus (or deficit).

settling with Switzerland were not sufficient to go round: the Swiss franc became a hard currency—so hard that it was reserved almost exclusively for making bilateral settlements with Switzerland.

The second strongest country in Table *X*, the United States, was prepared to accumulate gold without limit, but would not accept settlement in any national currencies except her own, unless they were unconditionally convertible into dollars.[1] However, the rest of the world's official holdings of gold and U.S. dollars at the end of the war were about $20 billions, and in the course of the post-war period there were further immense supplies made available as the result of the output of new gold, the operations of the I.M.F., and compensatory official financing by the United States government. This last occurred under various guises, including the loan granted to the United Kingdom in 1946, contributions to U.N.R.R.A. and other relief organizations, credits extended by the Export-Import Bank, and Marshall Aid. Thanks to these supplies of gold and dollars, the United States' vast overall surplus was accommodated with a reduction of only about a third in the rest of the world's official reserves of these currencies.

Yet this draining of the rest of the world's means of settlement with the United States, modest though it was in relation to the United States' overall surplus, caused widespread anxiety and led to the adoption of drastic policies to prevent a more rapid depletion of reserves. Countries tried not to waste their gold and dollars in making payments whenever softer currencies, such as sterling, could be substituted. In consequence, dollars went out of use as a regular means of multilateral settlement except in the Dollar Area, comprising the United States itself and certain of our Intermediate Group of countries. In the remaining Intermediate countries, gold and dollars had to be used for settling with the Dollar Area, but otherwise were in only occasional use for making settlements.

It will be remembered that countries in our Intermediate Group were either surplus countries with bilateral deficits

[1] American Account sterling was accepted in the United States only by virtue of the British monetary authorities' undertaking to convert it into dollars on demand.

with the United States and Switzerland or deficit countries whose only appreciable bilateral deficits were with the surplus countries—in practice mainly with the United States. All of the countries in this group had therefore a strong motive for preferring to receive settlements almost exclusively in U.S. dollars. They differed however very greatly in their ability to exact dollar settlements from their customers. The ones that were members of the Dollar Area—namely Canada and the American Account countries—could all exact dollar settlements[1] by virtue of being exporters predominantly of commodities which are either important United States imports (e.g. wood pulp, sugar, bananas) or which were basic necessities which their customers would otherwise have had to buy from the United States (e.g. oil). The other Intermediate Group countries were exporters either of less essential foodstuffs and raw materials in which the United States was self-sufficient (e.g. meat, cotton) or of manufactured goods. There was little possibility, for example, of Argentina, Brazil or Belgium exacting payment in dollars for all their exports without suffering a very serious contraction in their trade. Most of the Intermediate Group countries outside the Dollar Area had to accept and accumulate soft currencies from at least some of their customers for at least some of their exports, but nevertheless constantly tried to exact gold or dollars wherever possible.

Within our Weak Group of countries, gold and dollars were scarcely used at all except for settling with Switzerland, the Dollar Area and, much less frequently, with the remaining Intermediate countries.[2] In the Weak Group, however, as within the Dollar Area, there was a widely accepted medium for multilateral settlement, which in this case was sterling. Within this group was the Sterling Area itself, most of the Transferable Account countries and many of the 'Bilateral' countries which enjoyed the most liberal facilities for 'administrative transferability'. This is not to say that sterling was the

[1]Settlements from the Sterling Area in the form of American Account sterling are dollar settlements at one remove, owing to the unconditional convertibility of such sterling.

[2]e.g. Belgium.

*only* means of settlement in use among the Weak Group of countries: there were, for example, a number of bilateral agreements not involving the United Kingdom and there were the Indirect Aid provisions of the two Intra-European Payments Schemes. Nevertheless it is clear that a high proportion of settlements was made in sterling.

The advantages of sterling as an international currency have already been considered, in general terms, in Chapter IX, but two aspects of this question are perhaps worthy of emphasis here, as being specially relevant to the post-war period. *First*, the United Kingdom herself, and the Sterling Area as a whole, would always accept settlement in sterling, and never attempted to exact gold or dollars for passing on in settlement to the Dollar Area. The Sterling Area's dollar deficit had therefore to be met almost entirely from the reserve held by the Area at the end of the war, from the Area's current output of gold, and from loans and grants from the United States and Canada. *Second*, though there were many countries weaker than the Sterling Area, their currencies did not to any appreciable extent displace sterling as a means of settlement. This was partly because some of the countries running deficits with the Sterling Area were never seriously short of sterling, thanks to the balances they accumulated during the war, and partly because the possible rivals to sterling did not inspire enough confidence to ensure their acceptability.

The shortcoming of sterling as an international currency was of course that, except for a brief period in 1947, 'weak' holders of sterling, other than the Sterling Area countries, were not permitted to transfer it to the Dollar Area or indeed to any of the countries outside the Weak Group. This shortcoming did not however prevent sterling from operating as an international currency within the Weak Group.

### *The International Transmission of Depressions*

This was not a serious question in the post-war period, which was characterized by an excess, rather than a deficiency, of effective demand. The only significant manifestations of inadequate demand were, as we have seen, in the United States, Switzerland, Belgium, Western Germany and Italy.

In all these cases, except perhaps the last, other countries were troubled by the international impact of the depressions, but almost without exception the ground for legitimate complaint was the adverse effect on the victim-country's balance of payments, not on its domestic prosperity.

The more likely problem in the post-war period was the opposite one of the international transmission of inflation. Here however the countries suffering from inflation were mainly forced by their limited liquidity to apply import restrictions and thus to restrain their excess demand from spilling over into other countries.

Only two cases have to be noted of countries having enough liquidity to permit them to 'export' their excess demand. The first is that of the countries which had accumulated large sterling balances during the war, but here the blocking of part of the balances kept the problem within bounds. Britain did indeed complain of the 'unrequited exports' which were being bought with 'old sterling', but on the balance-of-payments ground that such exports ought to have gone to hard currency markets, not on the ground that they should have been sold on the home market to combat inflation. The second case is that of the recipients of Marshall Aid, whose purchases in the United States would have aggravated an inflationary condition in the American economy, had such a condition existed. However the warnings which were issued on this score in the early days of Marshall Aid proved in the event to be largely unjustified, since despite the export surplus financed by Marshall Aid the U.S. economy always maintained a pool (and in 1949 a rather excessive pool) of unemployment.

A country which considered that it was importing inflation from abroad would be likely to turn to remedies in the form of expedients which would (i) stimulate its imports or (ii) reduce either the volume of its exports or the home-currency earnings of its export producers. Such expedients would comprise mainly the reduction of restrictions on the country's imports, the appreciation of its currency, the imposition of export quotas and the levying of export taxes. Two of these devices, currency appreciation and export taxes, were adopted by a number of countries specializing in the export of primary commodities,[1] the prices of which were often extremely high in the post-war period, but it is difficult to say how much of the intense demand for most of these commodities could reasonably be attributed to 'inflation', as distinct from mere 'prosperity', or alternatively to stockpiling, in the importing countries.

As for export quotas, the industrialized countries limited exports of particular commodities, but (apart from restrictions imposed for strategic reasons) the range of goods involved was narrow, being confined mainly to coal and steel. The remaining expedient, a removal of import restrictions, was used (alas) only very infrequently. It would thus seem that generally speaking countries did not in fact commonly adopt expedients designed to fight inflation at home caused by inflationary conditions in other countries. This does not of course prove that they did not suffer inflation at home brought about in this way, but it surely suggests that such suffering was not intense and widespread.

[1]Canada, Sweden and New Zealand appreciated their currencies. Various countries levied export taxes—e.g. Malaya's tax on rubber. In other cases a government or producers' agency was given a monopoly of exports and levied what was in effect an export tax. This applied, for example, to Argentinian beef and West African cocoa.

CHAPTER XI

# SEPTEMBER 1949 AND AFTER

THE devaluation of sterling by about 30 per cent on the 18th September, 1949, was important not only in itself but because it touched off a wholesale readjustment of exchange rates throughout the Sterling Area (except Pakistan), throughout western Europe (except Switzerland), and in a number of other countries. It was 'the most extensive realignment of exchange rates ever carried out in a short period of time'.[1] Details are given in Table 15. As might be expected, the hardest of the currencies in use for making international payments, the U.S. dollar and the Swiss franc, were not devalued.

What were the motives which led to the devaluations, and in particular what were the motives which led the British Government to take the initiative? M. Gutt, then chairman of the I.M.F., regarded the devaluations as an attempt to close the dollar gap by the deficit countries 'adjusting their exchange rates in order to lower the prices of their goods and increase their sales to the western hemisphere'. Sir Stafford Cripps expressed a similar view on the day of the devaluation: 'With a low rate of exchange', he said, 'we can sell more of our goods abroad and so should be able to earn more dollars in total'. Nine days later however he was advising British exporters to 'maintain the dollar prices of our goods whenever possible', the implication being that a 30 per cent devaluation was worth while as a means of increasing dollar earnings only in the case of certain of our export products; in the case of other goods it would be better to offset the devaluation, partially or wholly, by maintaining their dollar prices.

In the event British manufacturers did not pay much heed to Sir Stafford's advice,[2] presumably because, as might have

[1]From M. Gutt's statement on behalf of the I.M.F.

[2]According to Table 7 on p. 11 of the E.C.E.'s *Economic Bulletin for Europe*, Vol. 2, No. 1, British export prices, measured in dollars, fell 28 per cent between the third quarter of 1949 and the first quarter of 1950.

## TABLE 15

DEVALUATIONS: 18TH SEPTEMBER, 1949, TO THE END OF 1949

| | Devaluation in relation to the U.S. dollar |
|---|---|
| | % |
| The Sterling Area except Pakistan | 30 |
| European Countries: | |
| Austria .. .. .. .. | 53[1] |
| Greece .. .. .. .. | 33 |
| Denmark, Finland, Netherlands, Norway, Sweden .. .. .. | 30 |
| France .. .. .. .. | 22[1] |
| Germany .. .. .. .. | 20 |
| Belgium .. .. .. .. | 13 |
| Portugal .. .. .. .. | 13 |
| Italy .. .. .. .. | 8 |
| Other Countries: | |
| Argentina .. .. .. .. | 47[1] |
| Egypt .. .. .. .. | 30 |
| Canada .. .. .. .. | 9 |

been expected, competition in the export trades was too fierce to allow dollar prices to be maintained when costs had risen only slightly in sterling (i.e. had fallen by nearly 30 per cent

[1]Austria introduced multiple rates in December 1949, so that the end-1949 rate is an average. The pre-devaluation rate for the French franc is taken as the mean of the basic and free official rates. Argentina changed some, but not all, of her multiple rates in October 1949, so that the percentage shown is necessarily approximate. See the 20th *Annual Report* of the B.I.S., p. 154.

measured in dollars). The effect of this large and almost general fall in the dollar prices of our exports was, as Sir Stafford appears to have feared, a disappointingly small increase in our dollar earnings. Indeed, but for the effect on our exports of the American business recovery after mid-1949 and for the speculative factors which (as we shall shortly see) depressed our exports before devaluation and stimulated them afterwards, it is very doubtful whether our dollar earnings would have increased at all. Thus from the point of view of permanently increasing our dollar earnings, devaluation was a failure. Moreover it was a costly failure, since if we put the reduction in our dollar prices at one quarter (and in practice it may have been rather more) an increase of one third in the volume of our exports would be taken up simply in maintaining our dollar earnings unchanged[1]—a most unwelcome burden on the already overloaded British economy.

On the side of imports, the British Government had already taken such wide powers of control (by trade restrictions, bulk purchase agreements, etc.) that devaluation was hardly needed as a means of reducing imports into the United Kingdom. Moreover, devaluation had the disadvantage, as the Government well knew, of raising the sterling prices of imports and consequently the British cost of living.

Thus far we have seen few advantages in devaluation from the British point of view, and though they may have allowed themselves a little unwarranted optimism it is doubtful whether members of the British Government really expected advantages in the directions we have so far considered. Where then did the advantages lie?

In the first place, in so far as the countries of the outer Sterling Area could be counted on to follow Britain's lead in devaluing, it was reasonable to expect that their dollar expenditure would be curtailed and the drain from the Sterling Area's dollar pool correspondingly reduced.[2] In theory the same

[1]If the prices of our exports changed in the ratio of $1 : \frac{3}{4}$, their volume would have to change in the ratio of $\frac{3}{4} : 1$ (i.e. of $1 : 1\frac{1}{3}$) in order to keep our total earnings unchanged.

[2]On the other hand, the outer Sterling Area's dollar receipts could not reasonably be expected to improve as the result of devaluation, since most of the products which the outer Sterling Area exports for dollars are primary

economy in dollar expenditure could have been achieved by more import restrictions in the outer Sterling Area countries, and this alternative had indeed been tried earlier in 1949, as the result of agreements reached in July at the meeting in London of the Commonwealth Finance ministers. But 'whether the independent members of the sterling area could in fact make the cuts through physical import controls, while dollar goods remained so attractively priced as they were at the old exchange rate, always seemed very doubtful'.[1] In the event the rather uncertain effect of these additional restrictions was strongly reinforced by the devaluation of sterling; the whole of the outer Sterling Area except Pakistan followed Britain's lead and there followed a spectacular reduction in dollar expenditure.

The other advantages to be gained from devaluation were (i) to put an end to the strong speculative position which had been built up against sterling, based on the belief that sterling would soon be devalued, and (ii) to stop the serious leaks which had developed in the British exchange control.[2]

The speculative position against sterling took two forms. The first was that importers were holding back from buying British goods, in the belief that devaluation would occur and that as a result British prices, measured in the importing countries' currencies, would decline. The second type of speculation against sterling was itself a leak in the exchange control, and consisted of the transfer of capital to the United States, to which reference was made in Chapter IX, motivated by the expectation that sterling would shortly be devalued. Where the capital transfers were effected by foreign owners of sterling, the expedients adopted for making the transfers commonly involved the diversion of Sterling Area exports

commodities, the demand for which is inelastic. That these earnings did improve after September 1949 must be attributed to other factors, notably the business revival in the United States and elsewhere, and the increase of stockpiling by the U.S. Government.

---

[1]From a very illuminating article by T. W. Kent on 'Devaluation One Year After', in *Lloyds Bank Review*, October 1950.

[2]See Sir Stafford Cripps's speech in the House of Commons on 27th September, 1949.

destined for the United States to a third country, whence the goods were reshipped to their American destination.

The other important leaks[1] in the British exchange control also involved 'third-country' trade: they arose partly on account of the disorderly sterling-dollar cross rates ruling in Paris (and in less important centres) and partly from the fact that many commodities could be bought more cheaply in the Dollar Area than elsewhere.

The devaluation of sterling served to stop the leaks in the British exchange control for three reasons. First, it led the French authorities to re-establish an orderly system of exchange rates.[2] Second, it served to reduce the price differentials that had grown up between the prices of certain commodities (e.g. cotton, wheat, wood-pulp, newsprint, sugar, copra, edible oils, tallow, aluminium and certain other non-ferrous metals) in the Dollar Area and the (higher) prices prevailing elsewhere.[3] Third, it led to a reversal of the speculative capital flow. In addition, once devaluation had occurred, the orders for British exports which had previously been held up in anticipation of devaluation came forward in a rush.

Why did other countries follow Britain's lead in devaluation? The speculation which had occurred against sterling had not spread to other currencies; indeed some of the countries which followed Britain's example had actually been receiving capital as part of the flight from sterling.[4] The loss of dollars through 'third country trade' is a valid ground for devaluation only in the case of a currency which is in extensive use as a means of international payment: hence this reason for devaluation cannot have been as strong for other currencies as it was for sterling, and indeed for most of the currencies which were devalued this particular consideration was largely irrelevant.

On the other hand, if the initiative in devaluation is taken by one country (Britain in this case) this may be accepted by her competitors as a reason for following suit, so as to redress the balance of competition. If Britain devalues, British exports

[1]Also described in Chapter IX.

[2]See above, p. 72.

[3]The examples quoted are taken from the *Economist* of 6th April, 1949, p. 721, 13th August, 1949, p. 370, and 20th August, 1949, p. 426.

[4]e.g. Australia.

will to some extent undercut Belgian goods in the Belgian home market and also in third markets such as the United States; hence (it may be argued) the Belgian franc must be devalued too. This line of argument was undoubtedly important in practice,[1] and may have been sound in the case of Belgium—a relatively small exporter and much less addicted to trade restrictions than most countries—but it is far from obvious that all Britain's competitors who devalued with her thereby benefited their dollar earnings.

Not only Britain's competitors, but also many of her main suppliers, took Britain's devaluation as a reason for following suit, so as to prevent the deterioration in the market conditions which their export-producers would otherwise have to face. If, for example, the Australian pound had not been devalued with sterling the Australian farmer would have found it impossible to earn the same number of Australian pounds in selling his produce on the British market, and the Australian devaluation may have been intended to prevent such a reduction in Australian prosperity. If this was the purpose of the Australian Government, the devaluation had nothing to do with correcting international disequilibria; moreover, since the Australian economy was at the time suffering from an excess, rather than a deficiency, of demand, it is not easy to sympathize with the case for devaluing as an anti-depression measure.[2]

The course of events since September 1949 has served to emphasize the disadvantages of devaluation, firstly because the Korean War and rearmament have disturbed the pattern of international disequilibria, and secondly because the burden of military preparations in western Europe feels heavier coming as it does on top of the export burden imposed by devaluation.

The result of the 1950 rearmament and stockpiling programmes in the United States was to increase the volume of

[1]For example, the French finance minister (quoted in *The Times* of 21st September, 1949) commented, 'The pound had to be devalued, but the rate chosen is a trade-war rate, which forces other countries on the defensive in regard to their economies and their international markets. These are the circumstances which have compelled the French Government to readjust the franc'. (Prior to September 1949, the French had argued that the value of sterling had been fixed unfairly high. See above, p. 72.)

[2]But, as *The Times* Australian correspondent commented, 'all political parties woo the farming vote'.

her imports and reduce the availability of goods for export. Moreover (and more importantly) the increased demand for primary commodities, not only in the United States but also in all the rearming countries, very greatly bid up their prices, and this affected the value of U.S. imports considerably more than of U.S. exports.[1] Thanks to these factors the dollar shortage seemed, in late 1950 and the first half of 1951, to be in the course of disappearing altogether.[2]

The subsequent reduction in stockpiling in the United States, and the mounting burden of defence expenditure in other countries, caused a serious reopening of the dollar gap in 1951, but the circumstances were such that no reputable economist thought a second round of devaluations to be the appropriate remedy. Indeed most commentators regarded the devaluations of 1949 as having increased, rather than diminished, the difficulty of restoring equilibrium in 1951; for the problem of the typical deficit country in 1951 was not to sell exports but to produce them, in the face of the insistent claims of rearmament.

So far however (i.e. to January 1952) none of the devaluing countries has retreated from the decisions taken in September 1949 with the exception of Canada, where in September 1950 the official par value which had been in force for twelve months was cancelled and the value of the currency left to 'be determined by conditions of supply and demand'.[3] Under these arrangements the Canadian dollar has appreciated to about the same value which it had in terms of U.S. dollars prior to September 1949. Although Canada has declared her intention to re-establish an effective par value 'as soon as circumstances warrant', her currency has now been 'free' for so long that

[1]See *The New Commodity Inflation*, by Oscar R. Hobson, in *Lloyds Bank Review* of April 1951.

[2]See the I.M.F.'s *Annual Report* for 1951, Chapter I.

[3]I.M.F. *Financial News Survey*, 6th October, 1950. This survey also indicates that complete *laissez-faire* is departed from at least to the extent necessary to ensure an orderly sterling-U.S. dollar cross rate. 'In order to ensure that rates for sterling in terms of Canadian dollars reflect an orderly sterling-U.S. dollar cross rate, the Canadian Foreign Exchange Control Board is prepared to buy and sell sterling against U.S. dollars . . . at the official rates. . . .' It has since been reported that the Canadian authorities have even been taking action to stabilize the value of their currency in terms of U.S. dollars (*Financial Times*, 15th May, 1951).

her policy cannot easily be reconciled with the spirit of the I.M.F. Agreement, with its emphasis on the advantages of stable exchange rates.

It might have been expected that the reduction in the dollar gap up to mid-1951 would have led to a decline in the severity of restrictions imposed on trade and payments. Admittedly the restrictions most directly affected would be those aimed specifically against the Dollar Area, but (since restrictions always tend to be applied indiscriminately) one might also have expected a decline in restrictionism in general. In practice, however, very little was done before the subsequent reopening of the dollar gap put an end to hopes of speedy progress. In particular, the Torquay conference of the Contracting Parties to the G.A.T.T. did not produce any spectacular reductions of tariffs.[1] The trade liberalization policy of the O.E.E.C. has not progressed much beyond the stage achieved at the time of the formation of the E.P.U. The I.M.F. has been critical of the payments restrictions imposed by its members,[2] but so far without much effect. All in all, the world of January 1952 is very much farther from free trade than it was even in the so-called protectionist era of the nineteen-thirties, and with the recent rapid worsening of the dollar position the present tendency is markedly for more, rather than for less, restrictions.

The rise in 1950 and early 1951 in primary commodity prices was, as we have just seen, a major factor in the temporary closing of the dollar gap, but on balance it has aggravated, rather than reduced, Britain's difficulties, for she now faces the problem of increased deficits with countries producing primary commodities, particularly with those which are members of the Sterling Area.[3] Some economists take the view that with

[1]See the article headed 'Good-bye to All G.A.T.T.', in the *Economist* of 21st April, 1951.

[2]Late in 1950 the Fund advised the G.A.T.T. that the restrictions on dollar imports which the U.K., Australia, New Zealand and Ceylon had imposed in 1949, prior to devaluation, should be progressively relaxed. (I.M.F. *Financial News Survey*, 12th November, 1950.) See also the Fund's second *Annual Report on Exchange Restrictions*.

[3]According to the White Paper on *United Kingdom Balance of Payments 1946 to 1950*, Cmd. 8201, Table 16, the U.K.'s sterling liabilities to other Sterling Area countries increased by £382 millions in the course of 1950.

the high level of primary commodity prices, Britain can avoid a large external deficit only by an appreciation of sterling; which would raise the prices of her exports in relation to those of her imports.[1]

Another recent problem in the field of international monetary affairs has been the development of a number of unduly large cumulative net positions (both debtor and creditor) in the E.P.U.[2] However, on this, and indeed on almost all the developments in the monetary field in the last year, detailed comment would be inappropriate, at any rate in a book of this kind, for it is so easy to see the recent past in false perspective. And it would be still more inappropriate, in these unsettled times, to hazard guesses about the future.

[1]See for example Mr. Harrod's article in the *Financial Times* of 12th December, 1951.

[2]See the article on the E.P.U. in the *Midland Bank Review* of February 1952.

# READING LIST

FOR an elementary exposition of that section of economic theory which deals with the factors affecting a country's balance of current payments, see Part Three of my *Wealth and Income* (Melbourne University Press, 1950) or R. F. Harrod's *International Economics* (Nisbet and C.U.P., 1941). More advanced students are strongly recommended to consult *Readings in the Theory of International Trade* (Blakiston, 1949), and J. E. Meade's *The Balance of Payments* (Oxford, 1951).

The charters or agreements which established the I.M.F., the G.A.T.T., the I.T.O., the I.E.P.S. and the E.P.U. are all published by H.M.S.O.; details have already been given in footnotes. Other literature about the work of these institutions include:


The I.M.F.'s own *Annual Reports*, and its *Annual Reports on Exchange Restrictions*.

The B.I.S.'s *Annual Reports*.

The *Annual Reports* of the Managing Board of the E.P.U., published by the O.E.E.C.

The Bank of England's annual *Reports* and the various White Papers on Sterling Agreements which are listed therein.

W. A. Brown, *The United States and the Restoration of World Trade* (Brookings Insitution, 1950).


There is a vast literature commenting on the I.M.F., and (to a much lesser extent) on the other institutions. Here is a very short selection:


Seymour E. Harris and others, *Foreign Economic Policy for the United States* (Harvard, 1948).

J. H. Williams, *Post-War Monetary Plans* (Blackwell, 1949).

R. F. Harrod, *The Life of John Maynard Keynes* (Macmillan, 1951).

J. W. Beyen, *Money in a Maelstrom* (Macmillan, 1951).

There is an enormous flow of official literature, mainly periodical, commenting on the course of events in the field of international monetary affairs. Here is a short selection:

The I.M.F.'s *Staff Papers*, its weekly *Financial News Survey*, its monthly *International Financial Statistics* and its *Balance of Payments Yearbook*, as well as the Reports already mentioned.

The B.I.S.'s *Annual Reports*.

The O.E.E.C.'s annual *Reports* and its two reports on *Internal Financial Stability*.

The E.C.E.'s annual *Economic Survey for Europe* and its quarterly *Economic Bulletin*.

The United Nations' *World Economic Reports*.

The U.K.'s annual *Economic Surveys* and the White Paper on the *United Kingdom Balance of Payments*.

The U.S. Department of Commerce's *Survey of Current Business* (monthly).

The U.S. *Federal Reserve Bulletin* (monthly).

The *Reports* of the National Advisory Council to the President of the United States.

# INDEX

For Product Safety Concerns and Information please contact our EU
representative GPSR@taylorandfrancis.com
Taylor & Francis Verlag GmbH, Kaufingerstraße 24, 80331 München, Germany

www.ingramcontent.com/pod-product-compliance
Lightning Source LLC
LaVergne TN
LVHW011133300926
849160LV00008B/639

* 9 7 8 0 4 1 5 6 0 7 4 1 4 *